Middle English Prose
Essays on Bibliographical Problems

Middle English Prose
Essays on Bibliographical Problems

edited by
A.S.G. Edwards
Derek Pearsall

GARLAND PUBLISHING, INC.
NEW YORK & LONDON
1981

Library of Congress Cataloging in Publication Data

Main entry under title:
Middle English prose.

    Papers delivered at the conference on Problems in
Middle English prose, held at Emmanuel College,
Cambridge, July 22 – 23, 1978.
    Includes index.
    1. English prose literature — Middle English,
1100 – 1500 — Criticism, Textual — Congresses.
2. Manuscripts, English (Middle) — Editing —
Congresses.   3. Cataloging of manuscripts —
Congresses.   4. English language — Middle English,
1100 – 1500 — Congresses.   I. Edwards, Anthony
Stockwell Garfield, 1942 –   II. Pearsall, Derek
Albert.
PR275.T45M5   828'.108'09   80-8595
ISBN 0-8240-9453-0

Printed on acid-free, 250-year-life paper
Manufactured in the United States of America

This volume is dedicated with
affection and gratitude to
Rossell Hope Robbins
to whom all students of
Middle English bibliography
owe a debt that can never be repaid.
In memory of his sixty-sixth birthday
celebrated at Emmanuel College, July 22, 1978

Contents

Introduction

This volume consists of papers delivered at the conference on "Problems in Middle English Prose" held at Emmanuel College, Cambridge, July 22–23, 1978. The conference was organized to launch the *Index of Middle English Prose*, and was the first large-scale meeting of contributors to and Editors and members of the Advisory Committee of the *Index*.

Proposals for an *Index of Middle English Prose* were first made by Rossell Hope Robbins, who, as Coeditor of the *Index of Middle English Verse*, was in the best position to recognize the need for and anticipate the problems of a companion *Index*. The importance of the project, as one of the outstanding desiderata of Middle English research, was recognized when the Mediaeval Academy of America gave its support in principle to the idea in 1975. The Cambridge Conference was the outcome of these beginnings, and was itself the beginning of one of the largest collaborative ventures in the history of Middle English scholarship. The project is particularly characterized by the high degree of cooperation it envisages between British and North American scholars.

The technical and logistic problems of presenting an *Index of Middle English Prose* are formidable, and have no doubt contributed largely to the long delay in providing such an essential research tool. The obvious first question, "What is Middle English prose?" is almost unanswerable in the abstract, and it will be clear from what follows that the *Index* will have to work on the basis of pragmatic and to some extent arbitrary answers to such questions. There was no difficulty, therefore, in deciding that the Cambridge Conference should be devoted to "Problems in Middle English Prose" and particularly to those problems of definition, classification, identification, and record that faced contributors and editors alike. The conference was thus truly a working conference, and all the papers were concerned with the practical problems presented by the *Index*.

Professor Rossell Hope Robbins begins by placing the whole project within the larger context of Middle English bibliography, drawing on the unique authority of his wide-ranging experience. The contributions of A.S.G. Edwards, R.E. Lewis, and A.I. Doyle, as printed here, are concerned with the systemic problems involved in the making of the *Index*. A.S.G. Edwards lays out the broad strategy for the project, while R.E. Lewis and A.I. Doyle address themselves to the more particular questions that contributors will have to answer when faced with large numbers of inadequately catalogued manuscripts containing large numbers of unidentified pieces of Middle English prose. The paper by Henry Hargreaves deals with recipes, which emerge as a test case both for identification and classification in the building of the *Index*. Anne Hudson and Valerie Lagorio deal with the problems presented within particular important genres and groupings of prose writings, while Elizabeth Salter gives an analysis of a particularly complex group of related texts, and an example of the kind of problems that the *Index* may be expected to clarify.

It should be stressed that no effort has been made to impose any uniformity of opinion upon the various papers. The aim of the conference was to explore different aspects of a particularly complex problem and to suggest some of their implications particularly in terms of method. Inevitably there were different views about aspects of the way in which we should proceed. Had there been complete unanimity there would have been little point in such a conference. We have allowed divergent viewpoints to stand, particularly since differences of opinion tend to reflect the importance of the issues involved. What was encouraging, however, was the broad degree of general agreement on procedures that did emerge in the papers and in the extensive discussion they generated. That was one of the most encouraging features of an extremely stimulating conference.

The *Index of Middle English Prose*, launched with such vigor and hope of prosperity, has had an auspicious beginning. The publication of the present volume will, it is hoped, consolidate this beginning, and strengthen the determination of the scholars involved to bring the project to a successful conclusion, as well as bringing it to the notice of the scholarly world at large, and providing a new view of one of the most important and certainly the most neglected areas of Middle English writing.

The Chairman of the Advisory Committee and the Executive General Editor, as organizers of the Cambridge Conference, would like to thank all those who contributed to the success of the conference, especially those whose contributions are not recorded here. They would offer particular thanks to Norman Blake and Laurel Braswell who chaired sessions at the conference; to Derek Brewer, Master of Emmanuel College, whose generosity in making the College available for the conference was appreciated no less than his own welcome presence; E.F. Foxton, Domestic Bursar, Emmanuel College; to Angus McIntosh and Kathleen Scott, who took the trouble to come to the conference and put the argument for a more generous concern, on the part of contributors, with matters, respectively, of dialectology and manuscript decoration; and to Rossell Hope Robbins, Honorary Advisory Editor to the *Index*, whose introductory address to the conference distilled the wisdom of a lifetime's research in the subject and whose presence gave the conference a sense both of history and mission.

In preparing this volume for final publication, we record with great sadness the death of Elizabeth Salter on May 7, 1980. She was one of those who took the initiative in encouraging the *Index*, and her presence at the Cambridge Conference was, as always, an inspiration to all who were there. Her death is an irreparable loss to our community of scholars and to the academic world at large.

A.S.G. EDWARDS
General Editor

DEREK PEARSALL
Chairman,
Advisory Committee for the *Index*

Middle English Prose
Essays on Bibliographical Problems

OPENING REMARKS

Revising my informal introduction for inclusion among the scholarly papers read at the international Cambridge Conference for the *Index of Middle English Prose* presents several unique problems. A formal paper, perhaps with added documentation, can be printed more or less as delivered--a finished product not needing further honing, a self-contained unit little affected by occasion or time. But an opening address is different: in the first place, nuances and implications are lost when speech is frozen on page, when the spontaneity and warmth between speaker and audience have been dissipated into *cold* type. Second, many points which might have been important, amusing, or revelatory at the time are no longer significant. The expressions of good will from the directors of fourteen medieval centers are now a matter of record; personal reminiscences of my years from 1934 to 1937 at Emmanuel College form a topic better suited to a still-to-be-written "Three Score Years and Ten." Third, some of the inside history of the genesis of the *Index* is of greater interest to those attending the Cambridge Conference than to the academic world at large.[1] Finally, a number of specific suggestions I raised about the theoretical direction as well as practical methodology have now been merged into the general guidelines for the project.

Consequently, in this revision I have followed Professor Edwards' suggestion and am concerning myself with placing this project in the recent context of Middle English bibliography.

Some kind of catalogue of works in Middle English prose has clearly been a desideratum for a long time. Compared to the present state of research in Middle English verse, research in Middle English prose is sixty years behindhand. We work under the scholarly handicaps of the year 1914.[2]

Medievalists are now reasonably familiar with Middle English verse. This awareness is due largely to *The Index of Middle English Verse* (hereafter *IMEV*), which Carleton Brown (posthumously, alas) and I published in 1943,[3] and to the *Supplement to the Index* in 1965.[4] *IMEV* grew out of Brown's early research, which bore fruit in 1916 with the first volume of his *Register of Middle English Religious and Didactic*

Verse,[5] a bare Handlist, giving only the manuscript, foliation,
title or brief description, and first line. Four years later,
in 1920, Brown rearranged this material in a second volume, an
alphabetical index, each entry listing the first line, the
title or brief description, form, manuscript and foliation, and
editions. Reference to Volume II spared any would-be editor of
a Middle English religious poem the many years it would otherwise have taken to conduct a comprehensive canvas of likely
manuscripts just to make sure all the texts were established.

Carleton Brown's *Register* first brought to the editing of
texts a sense of professionalism and thoroughness previously
lacking. References to the *Register* (1920) soon started appearing in EETS editions, first in 1921, then in 1926, 1927,
1928, 1930, 1931, 1933, and 1935. References to *IMEV* (1943)
were considerably delayed by World War II and its aftermath,
so that the first acknowledgements came only in 1956 and 1959.
The stimulus of both *Register* and *IMEV* is more clearly seen,
however, in the numerous editions of shorter poems in articles
in learned journals.

For nearly six decades, scholars have exploited this poetic
warehouse, so that now very little Middle English verse remains
unpublished. As a result, editors have been turning to prose
texts, as recent EETS publications indicate. In the past
twenty years, out of thirty-four volumes, sixteen have consist-
ed of prose works; but in the first twenty years of the
Society's existence (1864-1884), of the eighty published, only
thirteen were in prose. The publication of the *Index of Middle English Prose* will usher in a second golden age of medieval
studies.

Towards the realization of the final goal, Stage 3 as
Professor Edwards has termed it, two subordinate stages are
scheduled: Stage 1, an index of published prose, and Stage 2,
a series of detailed Handlists of prose items by manuscript.

Stage 1, the list of prose texts already in print, is
valuable for two reasons: for scholars compiling the Handlists
of manuscripts on location, it may help identify a prose text
with which they are not acquainted; and for other scholars it
provides a convenient ad hoc catalogue which will anticipate
some of the functions of the final first-line *Index* (Stage 3).[6]

Stage 2 will comprise the numerous fascicles listing the
prose items in the various collections of manuscripts. To me,
this preparatory research from which the *Index* will be con-
structed is the most important and most enduring part of the
entire project, if for no other reason than that if some
editor slights his task, or neglects to record adequately all
the prose in his assigned manuscript collection, the value of
the final *Index* will be so much lessened. The strength of the
chain lies in its weakest link. There is also a more important

reason, to which I will refer later.

Stage 1 is clearly pro tempore. But Stage 3 is also ephemeral, programmed for obsolescence. When, as we all hope and expect, the prose texts to be listed therein have been edited and published, the usefulness of the *Index* as a research tool will wither away. Such was the fate of the verse indices: the *Supplement* was remaindered, and although *IMEV* is still backlisted by the Modern Language Association, it is useless without the *Supplement*.

From time to time, scholars discover "new texts" not found in the *Supplement*, such as proverbs, scraps, tags from sermons, very few exhibiting any literary merit and very few longer than twenty lines.[7] For all practical purposes, therefore, *IMEV* and the *Supplement* were exhaustive and complete. And because of this, the current project of the MLA Middle English Division, the *Manual of the Writings in Middle English 1050-1500*,[8] has replaced *IMEV* as the major research tool. The *Manual* embraces both verse and prose, but even for Middle English verse the *Manual* is more up to date and far more comprehensive: it includes a description of the contents of the item, an account of the major criticism, along with facts on the dialect, date, form, author, and history; and furthermore, it includes a full classified bibliography. As a specimen, I append one of the shortest entries (purposely chosen to conserve space) from my section on the Chaucerian Apocrypha in the *Manual* (Vol. 4, Section XI, p. 1090):

THE TEN COMMANDMENTS OF LOVE [40], fourteen rime royal stanzas, in two late manuscripts, Trinity Cambridge 599 and Fairfax 16 (added in seventeenth-century hand), first printed by Stow in 1561, and reprinted until 1810. Probably no earlier than 1500; certainly (as the hand shows) later than Skeat's 1450. Brown-Robbins, no. 590.

After two introductory stanzas, the poet instructs ladies to observe the Ten Commandments of courtly love. It thus relates to the Statutes for Women in [37], which the poet there is forbidden to read.

Exhibit (1) good faith, (2) intention to please, (3) discretion in assignation, (4) patience, (5) secretiveness, (6) prudence in good judgment, (7) constancy, (8) pity, (9) moderation in talking, and (10) mercy.

The piece concludes with a two-stanza Envoy: Accept, lady, this 'balade' even though the devoted writer is devoid of literary skill.

In spite of its appeal to *The Romaunt of the Rose*, it is not dependent on it and can be linked only in a very general way to the commandments.

The bibliographical references come on page 1300:

> [40] THE TEN COMMANDMENTS OF LOVE
> *MSS.* 1, Bodl 3896 (Fairfax 16), ff 184-186b (added in
> 17 cent hand on blank leaves); 2, Trinity Camb 599, ff
> 109a-110a (1500-25).
> Brown-Robbins, Robbins-Cutler, no. 590.
> *Editions.* Note: See sections III and IV above for full
> bibliographical statement of the early editions here
> listed.
> Stow, Chaucer, 1561, f cccxliia.
> Speght, Chaucer, 1598, f 342a.
> Urry, Chaucer, 1721, p 554.
> Bell J, Poets of Great Britain, 1782, 13. 117.
> Anderson, British Poets, 1793, 1. 582.
> Chalmers, Eng Poets, 1. 560.
> Robbins, SL, p 165.
> *Date.* Oxf Ch, 7. xix; Skeat Canon, p 122 (corrected by
> Hammond, p 334).
> *Literary Relations.* Seaton, p 383.
> *General References.* Neilson, p 207.
> *Bibliography.* Hammond, p 457.

For comparison, here is the information in No. 590 taken
from *IMEV*:

> Certes fer extendeth my Reason
> 'The X Commaundments of love'--fourteen stanzas rime
> royal including Envoy.
> 1. Bodl 3896, f. 184a; 2. Trinity Camb. 599, f. 109a.
>   2. Stowe, *Chaucer* 1561; repr. Chalmers, *Eng. Poets*,
>   I. 560-1.

The *Supplement* added the following information:

> Speght, *Chaucer*, 1598 (STC 5077); Urry, *Chaucer*, 1721,
> p. 554; Bell, *Poets of Great Britain*, 1782, XIII. 117;
> Anderson, *Poets of Great Britain*, I. 582; 1. Robbins,
> *Sec. Lyrics*, pp. 165-8.

If a student wishes to get information about *The Ten Commandments of Love*, it is obvious that he will go, not to *IMEV* and
its *Supplement*, but to the *Manual*. For research workers the
superiority of the *Manual* over *IMEV* is evidenced even more
graphically by the longer entries of Section XI, like *The
Court of Love* or *The Isle of Ladies*.
     But--and what a pregnant "but" this is--without *IMEV* and
the *Supplement*, the *Manual* (so far as it relates to verse)

would not have been possible. One can see the aging and ultimate death of a comparable bibliographical tool, not based on
manuscripts, the original 1916 *Manual*, hailed so highly in its
lifetime, compiled single-handedly by John Edwin Wells.[9] Wells
depended entirely on printed editions, and consequently his
work was out of date before it came off the press; Wells had
always to be adding Supplements to include new texts that kept
on being published. And in so far as the new MLA *Manual*
(1962-) has not covered Middle English prose items still in
manuscript, so too its value will be diminished. Fortunately,
the *Manual* is being completed by scholars well versed in manuscripts, several of them in fact serving both *Manual* and *Index*
as editors or consultants.[10]

What is the *Index*? Obviously, an index of the writings in
Middle English prose. But what writings? Is the aim to produce a counterpart to *IMEV*, which attempted more or less successfully to catalogue *every* piece of Middle English verse
extant, every piece as short as a couplet or even a one-line
fragment of a popular song?[11] Should the *Index* attempt to include every piece of Middle English prose? Although this goal
may never be fully realized, I suggest we aim at it.

As Professor Edwards remarked at the Cambridge Conference,
the Contributing Editors of the *Index* are not compiling catalogues to replace the out-of-date, inaccurate, careless, and
limited catalogues that serve most collections. The reassurance
of first-class catalogues like those of Warner and Gilson for
the Royal collection[12] or Mynors for the Balliol College
collection[13] comes rarely, and the majority of Contributing
Editors will have to fumble with such rusty tools as the
catalogues for the Cotton manuscripts[14] or for Trinity College,
Dublin.[15] The validity of Professor Edwards' comment granted,
however, the question of the extent and comprehensiveness of
the *Index* goes unanswered.

On the general principles there is little occasion for
debate. The *Index* is primarily concerned with "literature"
rather than with "documents."[16] Literature is to be interpreted
generously: prose romances, certainly;[17] mystical and devotional
treatises and tracts, without doubt;[18] sermons,[19] saints' lives
and legends, polemical works, surely; chronicles and the *Brut*
are more than "documents." And what about travel literature,
medical treatises, alchemical texts?

Probably few medievalists would cavil at this inclusive
spread, which takes in functional as well as literary prose.
It is the specific application of the principles that raises
problems. *The Boke of St. Albans* is an important work and
should be listed; but should the "terms of association"
appear?[20] A prose exposition of the Pater Noster, which occu-
pies some 1,200 words, should be included; but what about the

innumerable Englishings that scatter dozens of manuscripts?[21]
Fortescue's *Governance of England*, Yes; Assizes of Bread,
possibly No.[22]

What principles of selection distinguish Fortescue from an
Assize? Is it the style of writing, the significance of the
subject, the importance of the author, the status of the
audience, the importance in later centuries? Or is it an
arbitrary factor such as length? Length might indeed be a
factor, for how important can a little item of three or four
lines be for the history of Middle English prose? Yet can our
decision be changed by the frequency of appearance, if those
few lines appear in half a dozen manuscripts?[23]

In actuality the principles governing what materials to
include may be decided by three quite extraneous considerations.

First is the time factor. How long can the publication of
the *Index*, Stage 3, be delayed by overmeticulous cataloguing
(Stage 2) by Contributing Editors? How many years can the
General Editor and his Coeditors wait for raw materials? Some
nice balance has to be struck on what is reasonable haste and
what is unreasonable overkill.

A second consideration: the fact that some fifty or more
Contributing Editors are preparing manuscript fascicles gives
another clue to the solution of the problem of what to include:
Diversity in Unity. In his guidelines (December 12, 1978),
General Editor Professor Edwards has given some criteria of
the *minimum* requirements:

> A number of requests were made at Cambridge for the
> *Index* to seek to assist the activities of various groups.
> Since these activities are tangential to the aims of the
> *Index* we do not wish to enjoin Contributing Editors to
> provide this information. But if Editors do have the
> opportunity and inclination and if they feel competent
> to do so, they may wish to record certain types of data
> concerning the manuscripts they examine.... It is
> obvious that to include all this is going to add to the
> burden of indexers considerably. But if Editors do feel
> inclined to record it, we will make available an addi-
> tional form sheet for them to use.

Professor Edwards was primarily concerned with descriptive
features of manuscripts (such as watermarks and names of
scribes), but I think this tolerant principle could be profit-
ably extended, as I shall later indicate. Some of the Contributing Editors who have had experience only with a few manuscripts
may find that recording even the minimal data presents a chal-
lenge. Those versed in quick examination of many manuscripts
will do more--those who have acquired over the years an instinct

for selecting the very manuscript which has ten pages of
English tucked away in the middle of a most unpromising pile
of Latin tracts, like a police dog detecting marijuana at a
baggage terminal or a humble pig rooting up its truffles.
Each Contributing Editor exercises some freedom of choice in
how to present his materials. After the first fascicles start
appearing--in miscellaneous order depending on the adequacy of
the catalogues, the number of manuscripts to be searched, the
complexity of manuscripts within the collection, as well as
the skills of the Editor--I think present hesitations will
seem less insuperable.

Third, and perhaps most significant, is a difference in
functions arising out of the disparate nature and function of
the several stages of the compilation of the *Index*. The functions of Stage 2 and Stage 3 are entirely different. From
one point of view, the mission of Stage 2 is to collect the
raw materials, which later will be sifted and winnowed to
select the alphabetized items for Stage 3; what is not used
can be discarded. From another point of view, however, the
latent objective of Stage 2 is to disseminate the manuscript
context in which the texts are found, and the "chaff" is
highly relevant. Unlike texts of later periods, every Middle
English work, whether verse or prose, must be considered in
its context within the manuscript, because the manuscript
gives indications of type of author, type of audience, and
type of use which elucidate the work. This critical approach
relies on these manuscript fascicles.[24] I would suggest that
these fascicles be designed to offer the greatest assistance
possible to *all* Middle English research workers, and that they
include all the material (even if much of it is not included
in Stage 3) a Contributing Editor is capable of handling. A
tremendous effort is being expended on this project, probably
the most determined and ambitious of any scholarly project of
this century, and while we are not aiming to include so much
information that further examination of manuscripts would not
be necessary--indeed, the opposite is true--I think we should
try to help scholars with many divergent interests. By our
work on the manuscript fascicles we should try as far as
possible to make it unnecessary for a researcher ever again to
face a *complete* canvas of several thousand manuscripts.[25]
Contributing Editors may even be listing data for some uses
which have not yet been contemplated.

This secondary function of Stage 2 is, in my opinion,
extremely important. It is these Handlists that will save the
Index from oblivion, from going the way of *IMEV*. While working
as pioneers on the last frontier of Middle English studies, in
Stage 3 we may be digging our own graves. But in death is our
immortality. Stage 3, when all the unpublished prose it lists

has been published, will be resurrected in some future MLA
Manual. On the other hand, the manuscript fascicles, by their
very nature, cannot ever be absorbed in any *Manual.* In this
respect, I think the disposition of Brown's *Register* encouraging.
As I have noted, Volume II (= Stage 3) was outdated by *IMEV*
and the *Supplement.* Yet recently a commercial publisher chose
to reprint the *Register* because Volume I (= Stage 2) was not
outdated. Sparse and barren as Brown's *Register* of manuscript
entries was, it still remains viable and helpful.[26] I can en-
vision a situation, some fifty years hence perchance, when the
Index too will have been remaindered, but when the fascicles
of the manuscript collections will be reprinted!

Though they deal exclusively with verse, throughout this
paper I have constantly been referring to the *Register*, *IMEV*,
and the *Supplement.* Most of the problems facing the *Index*
also cropped up in their preparation. Of course, the scope of
the *Index* is infinitely bigger, and consequently problems more
numerous.

As a case history which might be instructive for Contributing Editors, I would like to compare, drawing on the same
manuscript, the very restricted cataloguing adopted by Carleton
Brown in his *Register*, Volume I (1916), with the exhaustive
cataloguing of a doctoral candidate at Toronto (1975). I
doubt if any Contributing Editor will ever encounter a manuscript of such wide range as Bodleian 10234, Tanner 407, the
commonplace book of Robert Reynys of Acle, Norfolk.[27] The
difference in technique (that one scholar is looking for verse,
the other for verse and prose, is immaterial) is that Brown
restricts himself exclusively to items that would be included
in his alphabetical listings, whereas Dr. Cameron Louis included
all the miscellaneous material, much of which would not be
included in any alphabetical listing.

Here is Brown's listing (*Register*, I, 96-97):

Summary Cat. No. 10234   MS. Tanner 407   End XV cent.

    17b. [Maxims for daily conduct--eight lines.]
          Serue god treuly and ye world besely.
    18a. [Four lines.]
          There beth iij thynges that be moche of prys.
    18b. [Twenty-five 4-line stanzas--two lines written as
              one.]
          There ben iij poyntis of myscheff
          that arn confusion to many men.
    20a. [The children of St. Anne by her three marriages.]
          In the olde lawe in that lyff a man hyght ysakar.
    21a. [The Espousal of Mary and the Annunciation.]
          Souereynys and serys ȝyf it to be ȝour wille.

29b. [Two miracles of the B.V.]
[S]erys a merakyl or to I schal ȝou telle.
35b. [Signs of Death--eight lines.]
Whan þi hed quakyth *memento*.
35b. [Four lines.]
ffor loue of god and drede of peyne.
. . . .
36b. [Five lines.]
Drede god and alle thyng schal drede ȝow.
36b. [Eight lines.]
He that hath thoughte / ful in wardly and ofte.
See under: 'Who so him biþouȝte / inwardlich & ofte'.
. . . .
38b. [Eight lines.]
O Ihū mercy what world is thys.
. . . .
45a-47b. [The XV Signs of the Judgment; imperfect, begins
          with the eleventh day.]
The xj^te day schal come þounder lyth.
48b. [Twenty lines.]
Man in the Chirche not idyll thow stande.

The list has a number of faults, not to mention that the
majority of items are not identified. First, Brown overlooked
and omitted numerous religious and didactic poems (which were
not added until *IMEV* in 1943). For example:

10b. [*Index* 3443. Number of drops of Christ's blood.]
The novmbre of these dropes all I will reherse in
generall.
17b. [*Supplement* 1961.5. Simple prayer by Five Wounds--
one couplet.]
Lord Ihū Cryst goddes sone on lyve
haue mercy on vs for thy woundes fyve.
18a. [*Index* 1870. Four lines on Evils of Times.]
lex is leyd adoun.
32a. [*Index* 3456. Four lines of moral counsel.]
The rote of wysdam is god to drede.
44b. [*Index* 2380. Epilogue to a Miracle Play.]
Now wirshepful souereyns that syttyn here in sith.
52b. [*Index* 2504. Querela diuina.]
Man vnkynde / haue thow in mynde.

One can hardly fault Brown for omitting secular poems, for
they were omitted by design; but their inclusion would have
helped our understanding of the whole manuscript:

32a. [*Supplement* 1929.5. Three quatrains on King Arthur,
Charlemagne, and David.]
Lo Kyng Artour ful manly and ful wyse.

32b. [*Index* 3666.] IX wurthy.
  Ector de troye.
  Thow achylles in bataly me slow.
38b. [*Index* 1278. Trials of Old Men in Love--two
    quatrains.]
  I am olde whan age doth apele.
43b. [*Index* 1927. Poem on Delight.]
  Lo here is a ladde lyght / al fresch I ȝow plyght.
52a. [*Supplement* 35.5. Nonsense verses.]
  A fryer an heyward a fox a fulmer sittyng on a rewe.
  A tapster hym sittyng by to fythe þe cumpany þe best
    is a strewe.

On the other hand, Dr. Cameron Louis' dissertation was
intended to be comprehensive, and he included both Latin and
English texts, some 120 items in all. I append here, as an
example of what I consider the acme of manuscript cataloguing,
the first few items, omitting (for reasons of space) the Latin
pieces and the endings of the Middle English prose texts. This
list I have extrapolated from Dr. Louis' dissertation.[28] Not
all the items given below as part of a manuscript fascicle, it
must be emphasized, would appear in the *Index*, Stage 3. Items
4, 19, 22, 25, and perhaps 26 would not be listed; nor would
Item 15, which is in verse. Dr. Louis also included a description of the manuscript and a bibliography.

Bodleian Summary Catalogue 10234.   Tanner 407

Manuscript: 1. Paper (not ruled).
            2. Watermarks (six; cf. Briquet 189, 882, 1545,
               4649, 11258).
            3. Quires: nine (8 and 9 rearranged).
            4. Hand: late conservative Anglicana.
            5. Date: ca. 1470-1475 (one entry 1500).
            6. Scribe: Robert Reynys of Acle, Norfolk.
            7. Dialect: East Anglian.

Printed references:
  Bodleian Summary Catalogue, 1 (1953), xxx.
  Alfred Hackman, *Cat. Cod. MSS. Bibl. Bodl.*, 4 (1860), cols
    764-5.
  Brown, *Register*, 1 (1916), 96.
  Blomefield, *History of Norfolk*, 1 (1739).
  I.G. Calderhead, *MP* 14 (1916), 1-9.
  Brown, *Religious Lyrics XIVth Cent.*, 47, 72.
  Robbins, *Secular Lyrics*, 20, 37, 44, 73.
  C.L.S. Linnell, Commonplace Book of Robert Reynys of Acle,
    Norfolk Archaeology 32 (1949), 134-6.
  Davis, *EETS* SS 1, cxx-cxxiv, 121-3.
  Woolf, *English Religious Lyrics* (1968), 376.

1. ff. 1r-7v   [Notes on regulations and controls on food,
                Latin with a few English inserts. Cf. *Statutes
                of the Realm*, 1 (1810), 199-200, and elsewhere.]
                Statutum panis et seruisie.
   f. 6v [About ten English lines at end of Latin.]
      Bred that is sysed: the ferthyng wastell, the ferthyng
        symnell
   f. 7r Assyse of Bred.
      It is for to haue in mynde þat þe assyse of bred shall
      be taken after þe myddes prys of whete and neyther of
      the best ne of þe worst, and þat þe wyte schall not be
      chaunged but at vi d. incresynge of sale of a quarter
      of whete of disencresynge.... [23 lines.]
   ff. 7r-7v Assyse of Ale.
      It is to wete þat whan a quarter of whete is solde for
      iii s. or for xl d., and barly for xx d. or for ii s.,
      and otys for xvi d., þan may 'well' the breweres selle
      in citie and burgh ii galounys of good and conable ale
      to drynk for i d.... [32 lines.]
      Item, wyte ȝe þat þe brewster shall not encrese or
      dysencrese þe assyse of ale in xii d. hyeng or lowyng
      in the price of a quarter of malt but a ferthyng etc.
4. f. 8r   [Local:] Memorandum of the great dredfull
               ffyer in Acle 1475. [4 lines ending with
               exact date in Latin.]
8. f. 8v   [Formulary for administering oaths to jurors
               in criminal cases, civil cases, and instructions
               to jurors in debt cases.] Ad faciendum
               iusiurandum ad inquisitionem.
      ȝe scholn soth seyn of alle maner articules þat schal
      be put to ȝow here of þe Kyngis behalfe and trew
      verdite make.... [10 lines.]
      De iuratoribus inter partes et partes.... Of how
      many articules ȝe schulne soth seyn.... [10 lines.]
      And 'if' he be detour to hym as he beryth him on hande
      or in partye lesse or more, ȝif hym his dette and
      awarde for his dampniage. And ȝif he be nouth gylty
      aqwyte hym.
10. f. 9r   [The manner of doing homage and fealty.]
      Homage: When a freman schall do his homage to his chef
      lord.... [9 lines.]
      Ffewte: When a freman schal do fewte to his lord, he
      schal ley his rygth hand on the boke.... [5 lines.]
15. f. 10v   [Verse: *IMEV* and *Supplement*, 3443.]
      [The number of the drops of Christ's blood--6 lines.]
      The novmbre of these dropes all
16. f. 10v   [Directions for finding changes of the moon.]
      To knowe on what day chaunge 'of' the mone schal be, first
      loke in þe kalender wher ȝour prime is.... [6 lines.]

19. f. 11r   [Terms for food rents. Other examples in
                W.H. Hart and P.A. Lyons, eds., *Cartularium
                Monasterii de Rameseia*, RS 79, 3, 160-2.]
      Memorandum: To the last day of þe xl dayes longen c
      ml., iii ml. and viii c and xl semes of whete
      strekyn.... [7 lines.]
20. f. 11r   [Charges to peace officers. Other oaths in
                Smith, *English Guilds*, pp. 316-7.]
      Charge to the Constabelis
      ʒe schul first pryncypaly take hede þat þe pees be
      kepte in ʒoure towne.... [25 lines.]
      Charge to the watche
      ʒe schal þis nyʒght folwyng ... make and kepe watche
      thrugh this towne withinne the boundys of ʒour
      watche.... [30 lines.]
21. ff. 11v-13r [Directions for blood-letting. Cf. C.H.
                Talbot, *Medicine in Medieval England* (1967),
                p. 130.]
      Ysodor seyth be auctoryte of Ypocras þat þer arn iii
      dayes þat no man owyth to be lete blood....
      Her may a man knowyn in what monyth and what houre of
      þe day is best bledyng for dyuers complexiouns....
      [80 lines.]
22. f. 13r   [Local: Various local taxes at Acle. Personal
                title, Peters Pence (Rome-shotʒ), some kind
                of royal levy.]
25. f. 14r   [Local: Lands of the Manor of Acle, list and
                values.]
26. f. 14v   [Concords. Cf. *GCPRO* 1, 135-6; Holdsworth,
                pp. 237-45.]
      How many concordis ben in your gain? [7 lines.]
29. f. 15r   [Onimancy: Procedure for Divination. Cf. Lewis
                Spence, *Encyclopedia of Occultism* (1960),
                p. 307.]
      Take on chyld of yonge age, þat is betwyxen vii and
      xiiii, and in the sonne set hym betwyxen þi leggis.
      And than knytte a red sylke thred abowte his ryght
      thombe iii, and scrape hys nayle wele and clene....
      [20 lines.]

      Finally, might I suggest how helpful it would be to those
medievalists whose needs are not sustained by Stage 3 but who
are very much interested in the non-entry material of Stage 2
if each Contributing Editor made an index of the significant
topics dealt with in the manuscripts in his assigned collection,
not only titles and authors, but minor topics, such as pen
trials, charms, lists of articles of belief, mottoes. From
Dr. Louis' dissertation, I have compiled the following index
to indicate the potential usefulness of such indices.

Tanner 407   Subject and Title Index (numbers refer to items)

Might I reemphasize that this manuscript, Tanner 407, is extremely involved, and very few Contributing Editors will find one of similar complexity. This subject and title index, of course, could be considerably extended (e.g., by including the verse items).

I will end these "Opening Remarks" with a direct quotation from my speech, which needs no revision, because (I am told) it successfully set the tone of the Cambridge Conference of 1978:

> The need for full scholarly cooperation is essential, and I hope this meeting will cement such amicable unity

on the part of all scholars of good will to the end that
the little infant *Index*, conceived longer than any ele-
phant, swaddled for many years, crawling a little in
1977, now standing on its feet in 1978, will grow and
prosper and romp home to an early and fruitful maturity.
Only with sincerity, with devotion not to individual
kudos but to the common profit, with dedication to the
point of sacrifice, and with a unified determination for
excellence, can this project, now undertaken, be brought
to the successful conclusion we all desire.

Rossell Hope Robbins
State University of New York at Albany

NOTES

1. For the curious, this "inside history," with other
materials, was recorded on several tapes by Dr. Michael
Korhammer in Munich, May 28 and June 2, 1977, and is now on
sealed deposit with the English Department, University of
Munich.

2. See *Supplement* (note 4 below): "The second half of the
[twentieth] century must inevitably be concerned with prose.
Much research has already been conducted on devotional writings,
but this is but a small part of all Middle English prose. The
same problems that faced the student of poetry before 1920 (and
1943)--namely, the need to spend years of preparatory research
examining catalogue after catalogue in the often vain hope
of establishing the texts--today face those students desirous
of working on Middle English prose. In my opinion, the preparation of the charts for these little sailed seas is the
greatest desideratum for Middle English studies--taking precedence even over exhaustive bibliographies, which can never be
definitive because they rely on printed editions" (p. xxiv).
See also "Mirth in Manuscripts" in *Essays & Studies*, n.s. 21
(1968), 14-20: "The most urgent of all Middle English projects
... is an index of ME prose, comparable to the index for the
verse" (p. 17 and n. 89).

3. Carleton Brown and Rossell Hope Robbins, *The Index of
Middle English Verse* (New York, 1943). The provisional title,
"The Manuscript Index of Middle English Verse," was reluctantly
discarded--see *Supplement* (note 4 below), p. xi.

4. Rossell Hope Robbins and John L. Cutler, *Supplement to
the Index of Middle English Verse* (Lexington, Ky., 1965).

      5. Carleton Brown, *A Register of Middle English Religious
and Didactic Verse*, 2 vols. (Oxford, 1916, 1920).

      6. In *Essays & Studies*, n.s. 21 (1968), 18, I broke down
the preliminary studies in some detail, giving Stage 1 as my
Part 5.   I discussed Stage 2 in detail, pp. 19-20: "Basic
Manuscript Research 1: Handlists of Manuscripts with ME Prose,"
giving highlights of suitable manuscripts from the B.L. Arundel
collection and hints to junior Contributing Editors.   The
second aspect of my "Basic Manuscript Research," Editions of
Middle English Prose Manuscripts, pp. 20-24, has already, in
the twelve years since it appeared, sparked a considerable
amount of new research, especially in Middle English sermons
and in commonplace books.   A few other aids are already published, keyed to manuscript investigation: Peter Revell,
*Fifteenth Century English Prayers and Meditations: A Descrip-
tive List of Manuscripts in the British Library* (New York,
1975), though it acknowledges in its preface (p. ix) both *IMEV*
and *Supplement*, fails to give the numerical references, and
apparently omits information available in those two works,
e.g., No. 145 is not identified as an extract from the *Pricke
of Conscience* (listed in *IMEV* as No. 3428 C); No. 204 omits the
Bodleian text (*Supplement*, No. 253); No. 34 does not identify
ff. 15v-19v as an extract from the *Revelations of St. Bridget*
(Book VII, cap. 7), though Revell enters the complete text
(Nos. 112-15); No. 280 is presumed to be a fifteenth-century
poem, but the hand is early sixteenth century, and the rubric
refers to the poem's being compiled by "elener percie,"
"ducissa Buckhammie."   This is Alianore, eldest daughter of
Henry Percy, 4th Earl of Northumberland, who married Edward
Stafford, 3rd Duke of Buckingham (1478-1521) only in 1500.   A
more ambitious work is that by P.S. Jolliffe, *A Check-List of
Middle English Prose Writings of Spiritual Guidance* (Toronto,
1974).   And see note 17 below for another useful Handlist.

      7. Some new classes of entries had been anticipated; see
Supplement, p. xxi.

      8. *A Manual of the Writings in Middle English 1050-1500*
(New Haven, 1967-).   General Editor, J. Burke Severs: Vol. 1
(1967), I.   Romances; Vol. 2 (1970), II. Pearl Poet, III. Wy-
cliff and his Followers, IV. Translations and Paraphrases of
the Bible and Commentary, V. Saints' Legends, VI. Instructions
for Religious.   General Editor, Albert E. Hartung: Vol. 3
(1972), VII. Dialogues, Debates, and Catechisms, VIII. Thomas
Hoccleve, IX. Malory and Caxton; Vol. 4 (1973), X. Middle Scots
Writers, XI. The Chaucerian Apocrypha; Vol. 5 (1975), XII. Dramatic Pieces, Folk Drama, XIII. Poems Dealing with Contemporary
Conditions; Vol. 6 (1979), XIV. Carols, XV. Ballads, XVI. Lyd-
gate; Vol. 7 (1980), XVII. Lyrics.   In December 1978, the MLA

Editorial Committee of the Middle English Division decided to
delete the section on Chaucer to avoid multiplicity of efforts.
Writing before the publication of the first volume in 1967, I
miscalculated the importance of *IMEV* and the *Supplement* as the
raw material on which the poetic entries for the *Manual* could
be based; consequently the fears I expressed in *Essays & Studies*,
n.s. 21 (1968), 17 n. 90 have not materialized, and the *Manual*
has assumed first place.

9. John Edwin Wells, *A Manual of the Writings in Middle
English 1050-1400* (New Haven, 1916); *First Supplement* (1919);
Second Supplement (1923); *Third Supplement* (1926); *Fourth Supplement* (1929); *Fifth Supplement* (1932); *Sixth Supplement* (1935);
Seventh Supplement (1938); *Eighth Supplement* (1941); *Ninth Supplement*, by Beatrice Daw Brown, Eleanor K. Henningham, and
Francis Lee Utley, revised to December 1945 (1951). Wells'
aim was extensive, but circumscribed by his methodology: "This
manual makes the first attempt to treat all the extant writings
in print, from single lines to the most extensive pieces, composed in English between 1050 and 1400" (p. vii). See also
note 11 below.

10. This scholarly cooperation has also been extended to
another major project, where early English literature is but
one part of a much larger whole, *Lexikon des Mittelalters*
(Munich and Zurich, 1978-). Many scholars, editors or advisers
of the *Index*, are preparing entries for it under my direction,
as *Herausgeber* for Altenglische Literatur and Mittelenglische
Literatur.

11. *IMEV*: "In this Index we have before us all Middle
English verse" (p. x). For broadening of criteria for inclusion of further texts see *Supplement*, p. xiv.

12. Sir George F. Warner and Julius P. Gilson, *Catalogue
of Western Manuscripts in the Old Royal and King's Collections*
(Oxford, 1921), 4 vols.

13. R.A.B. Mynors, *Catalogue of the Manuscripts at Balliol
College Oxford* (Oxford, 1963).

14. *A Catalogue of the Cotton Manuscripts deposited in the
British Museum* (London, 1802).

15. T.K. Abbot, *Catalogue of the Manuscripts in the Library
of Trinity College Dublin* (1900).

16. Yet Wells included "documents," and devoted a special
section to them (Chapter X, Part 9). It *is* useful to know,
for example, that wills in English were written between 1050
and 1097, that a proclamation of Henry II was issued in English
in 1258 along with Latin and French versions, and that the

first petition in English to Parliament came in 1386 (although it did not change the French pattern for several decades). In general, if the *Index* gets diverted into essentially historical documents, its completion may be delayed. But a "historical" item that lists the badges of the great magnates (like Digby 84) is very useful when editing *Historical Poems of the XIVth and XVth Centuries* (New York, 1959). It seems to me that if the *Index* does not include such pieces, the MLA *Manual* must collect them--and since the majority of such "documents" are still unpublished, collecting such entries will mean someone has to do our present canvas all over again. This is one of the reasons why I urge Contributing Editors to err on the side of inclusiveness. I think their approach should be, "When in doubt, include," rather than "What can we exclude?" The General Editor and the Advisory Committee will do the excluding; the fascicles can be generous and (so far as possible) list *all* prose items.

17. For a valuable catalogue of romances in verse and prose with good descriptions of the manuscripts, see Gisela Guddat-Figge, *Catalogue of Manuscripts Containing Middle English Romances* (Munich, 1976), Münchener Universitäts-Schriften Philosophische Fakultät, Band 4. In addition to the romances, Dr. Guddat-Figge lists all the other items in each manuscript.

18. For an early plan for classification, see Norman F. Blake, "Varieties of Middle English Religious Prose," in *Chaucer and Middle English Studies in Honour of Rossell Hope Robbins*, ed. Beryl Rowland (London, 1974), pp. 348-56. For current information on Middle English mystical literature, consult *14th-Century English Mystics Newsletter*, ed. Ritamary Bradley and Valerie M. Lagorio, Vol. 1 (1975)-date.

19. For current information on Middle English sermons, consult *Medieval Sermon Studies*, ed. Gloria Cigman, No. 1 (1977)-date.

20. 1486, repr. Wynkyn de Worde, 1496; modern ed. William Blades, *The Boke of St. Albans* (London, 1881), facsimile. For detailed bibliography and full discussion of texts and variants see Rachel Hands, *English Hawking and Hunting in "The Boke of St. Albans"* (Oxford, 1975). Terms of association are listed on p. lxviii.

21. Thornton, f. 209b, printed C. Horstman, *Yorkshire Writers: Richard Rolle of Hampole* (London, 1895), I, 261-64. The direct translations of the Pater Noster, in prose and verse, are too numerous even to attempt to catalogue here.

22. Sir John Fortescue, *The Governance of England*, ed. Charles Plummer (Oxford, 1885). For Assizes of Bread see Tanner 407, f. 7^v.

23. E.g., medical receipts, discussed by Professor Henry
Hargreaves.

24. For an example of how knowledge of the sixth manuscript
reverses the impression given by the other five manuscripts,
see my article "The Middle English Court Love Lyric," in *The
Interpretation of Medieval Lyric Poetry*, ed. W.H.T. Jackson
(London, 1979).

25. Cf. note 16 above. In my opinion, Contributing Editors
should not pass over items that do not appear to have immediate
relevancy, such as arabic or roman numerals, pen trials,
doodlings and scribbles on flyleaves. For example, here are
some Middle English prose items I would like to see included in
the "manuscript bibliographies" if not necessarily in the alphabetized first-line entries: Coronation ceremonies for various
rulers of Europe (Arundel 149), Patterns for working of lace
(Arundel 276), Cookery recipes (Arundel 334), Order for Shooting
with the Crossbow (Arundel 359), Priory of St. Bartholomew at
Smithfield (Cotton Vesp. B.ix), Claims of Edward IV to the
kingdoms of Britain, France, and Spain (Cotton Vesp. E.vii),
Menstruation (Egerton 827), Vision of St. Matilda (Egerton
2006). The list could be extended indefinitely. Some amusing
prose entries are noted in *Essays & Studies*, n.s. 21 (1968),
1-28.

26. I never made any effort to compile a handlist of the
contents of the manuscripts I examined in preparing *IMEV* and
the *Supplement*. I started by inserting pages into my copy of
Brown's *Register*, Vol. I; my working copy now consists of
notes occupying four comparably sized volumes.

27. Other excellent editions of commonplace books include
Karl Reichl, *Religiose Dichtung im englischen Hochmittelalter*
(Munich, 1973), Münchener Universitätis-Schriften Philosophische
Fakultät, Band 1; A.G. Rigg, *A Glastonbury Miscellany of the
Fifteenth Century* (London, 1968); Nita Scudder Baugh, *A Worcester
Miscellany* (Philadelphia, 1956); Rudolf Brotanek, *Mittelenglische
Dichtungen, aus der Handschrift 432 des Trinity College in
Dublin* (Halle, 1940).

28. I had the pleasure of being External Examiner for
Cameron Louis at Toronto University. A version of the dissertation has been published by Garland Publishing (New York,
1980).

TOWARDS AN INDEX OF
MIDDLE ENGLISH PROSE

My title, unambitious as it is, was in fact chosen with
some care. It conveys, I think, certain distinctive features
of the *Index of Middle English Prose* as it is at present conceived. It suggests a sense of direction--without being at
all specific about where one is proceeding from or going to.
It conveys (or rather, it is intended to convey) a sense of
purposeful inexactitude which accurately reflects the present
state of our project. Indeed, as I will try to show, it must
be virtually a necessary precondition of it. We are embarking
upon a project without precedent in its scope in Middle English
studies. And we will often find ourselves proceeding over
terrain of extraordinary difficulty without the benefit of
even the most rudimentary of sketch maps. In the following
brief comments, I would like to outline the circumstances that
have brought us to the very edge of this scholarly Matto Grosso
and to suggest some of the more obvious difficulties that are
likely to confront us as we prepare to hew our way through the
undergrowth.

I

The call for an *Index of Middle English Prose* has been
growing steadily for over two decades now as scholars have
grown to feel, with increasing urgency, the need for some
bibliographical tool to assist them in this most complex of
areas. It is appropriate that Professor R.H. Robbins, Co-
Compiler of the *Index of Middle English Verse*, should have
been the most frequent projector of a comparable volume for
prose texts.[1] But his frequent exhortations have not tended
to produce much significant action. Such advances as have
taken place in the subject recently have tended to be of an
unsystematic and imperfect kind. Most notable has been the
work of Peter Jolliffe, who has produced a preliminary bibliographical survey of some aspects of Middle English prose which
is of considerable value.[2] Helpful but of less value have

been the various fascicles of the revised *Manual of the Writings in Middle English* (regrettably few in number)[3] which have so far appeared, or Peter Revell's study of Middle English prayers in the British Museum.[4] And inevitably this paucity of bibliographical research has inhibited editorial activity in this field. Although important prose texts have continued to appear, we still lack adequate editions of a great deal of the corpus. Nor have any of the obvious institutions made any serious efforts to implement the creation of such an *Index* as we propose.

It is therefore not surprising that so little progress has been made towards organizing and implementing a reliable bibliographical account of Middle English prose. Only very recently has the situation shown any signs of amelioration. It is both appropriate and predictable that Professor Robbins should have been the catalyst in the change. In December 1975, at the San Francisco meeting of the Modern Language Association, he and I met and agreed that work on a prose *Index* should no longer be delayed. We agreed, in principle, to pool our energies to work towards the creation of such a tool.

It was, of course, clear from the outset that our work would entail collaboration among a large number of scholars. We first attempted to determine the degree of support for such an *Index*. A preliminary meeting at the New Orleans Meeting of the Mediaeval Academy in March 1976 indicated the interest of a number of North American scholars. But an obvious pre-requisite for the success of our plans was the participation of British scholars who had far greater access to the bulk of the material. During the autumn of 1976 while I was in England a number of senior British medievalists--Derek Pearsall, Elizabeth Salter, Norman Blake, Derek Brewer, and Ronald Waldron--offered their advice and support. We met together informally to discuss the concept of the *Index* at the Centre for Mediaeval Studies at York on January 8, 1977. At this meeting we were able to clarify priorities in the planning of our work and to discuss basic problems of organization and methodology. Indeed, so much progress was made that we felt sufficiently confident to proceed to the next stage: the creation of an Advisory Committee of senior medievalists to provide guidance and academic credibility for our plans. We were able, during the first part of 1977, to add to the names of Blake, Brewer, Pearsall, Salter, and Waldron, those of Morton Bloomfield, Ian Doyle, E. Talbot Donaldson, Anne Hudson, Alexandra Johnston, Robert Lumiansky, Valerie Lagorio, Malcolm Parkes, and Siegfried Wenzel. A little later, Professor Robbins assumed the position of Honorary Advisory Editor to the *Index*. This collective support from the British and North

American scholarly communities provided the credibility and
expertise which enabled us to proceed to the development of
procedures for the implementation of the *Index*.

It is to these procedures that I now turn. The plans we
have formulated recognize the quite extraordinary complexity
of our task. They also recognize that there is no single way
of dealing with that complexity. Thus work will proceed in
several self-contained stages which will interlock to provide
the basis for a final, complete *Index*.

The first step will be the publication of a first-line
index to all Middle English prose published in printed texts
from 1476 to the present. This work will be the necessary
bibliographical underpinning to the project, by providing a
tool that will facilitate identification of texts. The value
of such an index is circumscribed for the purposes of identifying texts in manuscript, although we will attempt to list all
manuscripts known to us of any published works. Obviously our
work will be of no help to scholars confronted with works that
exist only in manuscript. But even to be able to confirm that
such is the case will be of some value, especially for the
scholar contemplating editorial work. Our first-line index--
which is being undertaken by Professors N.F. Blake, R.E. Lewis,
and myself--will offer a conspectus of the editorial and bibliographical states of the subject and aim to provide the
researcher with a clear sense of where he is about to enter
terra incognita.

At the same time we are also initiating a series of bibliographical catalogues to deal in detail with particularly complex generic or authorial problems. A catalogue of Middle
English grammatical texts, compiled by David Thomson, is already published (New York, 1979). Lister Matheson is advanced
on a detailed examination of the (roughly) 140 manuscripts of
versions of the prose *Brut*. We hope soon to assemble a team
of scholars to study the complexities of the 250-odd manuscripts
of the Wycliffite Bible. Other catalogues will (I hope) be
prepared in due course, of both problematic genres and particular authors--we need, for example, detailed up-to-date accounts
of the manuscripts of such writers as Trevisa, Rolle, and
Hilton. These catalogues will be independent, self-contained
works, but prepared under the auspices of the *Index* project
and involving the collaboration and support of all those
associated with it. They will enable us to assemble in detail
evidence for bibliographical conclusions which can then be
employed in the *Index* proper without impracticably extending
its bulk. It seems likely that a number of groups of texts
are going to present problems of manuscript interrelationship,
textual variation, and attribution which will require extensive
separate treatment before they can be satisfactorily indexed.

Concurrent as well with this activity will be the most crucial stage of the total project. This will be the preparation of a series of Handlists, tentatively titled "Bibliographical Handlists for an Index of Middle English Prose." Each one of these Handlists will be a detailed descriptive index of the prose in a major collection (or groups of smaller collections). Each will be published under the name of the compiler(s). They will not, of course, constitute the final *Index*, but they will provide much valuable material for it. And they will make portions of our work available for scholarly use substantially in advance of the finished *Index*--while affording us the opportunity to benefit from corrigenda and addenda before committing the final work to print. The benefits of this procedure will be readily apparent: error in the completed *Index* should be significantly reduced; it may prove possible, for example, through this interim phase to identify works which might be overlooked--for reasons to which I shall return; and individual compilers will have the appropriate recognition for their work in the form of separate publication.

There have been certain questions raised about this way of proceeding. Objections have been raised to indexing by collections and to the publication of interim research. It has been urged, for example, that we need generic indexes, not lists of prose by collection. Clearly, full lists of all extant sermons, romances, saints' lives, and the like are a prime desideratum of Middle English studies. But they follow from and cannot precede the full assembling of all extant materials and the preparation of satisfactory generic categorizations which we do not have for much Middle English prose.[5] In the meantime collection-by-collection examination is the most economical way (in terms of both time and money) of assembling that material.

There are cogent objections to the publication of interim research--the chief of them being simply that it *is* interim. Moreover, it introduces a cumbersome-looking step rather than focusing effort directly on the publication of the final work. Such objections fail, however, to grasp the full implications of the *Index* or of the time it will take to complete. It will be, I would guess, at least two decades before a definitive *Index of Middle English Prose* can appear, drawing upon the material of the assembled Handlists and the bibliography of published Middle English prose. This final *Index* will differ in some respects from the Handlists that precede it (I will return to this in a moment), and it will, of course, be supplemented by materials from (for example) smaller collections, and manuscripts in private hands or in various record repositories. But its prime intent will differ only in scale. It will aim to offer a cumulated listing of all known texts

of Middle English prose works insofar as it has been possible
to do so. The bulk and complexity of the material, not sloth
or incompetence, impose these demands of time upon us. And
the myriad pitfalls confronting the would-be bibliographer of
prose are so great in number and so various in kind that it is
necessary to proceed at every stage with a proper tentative-
ness. But it seems inappropriate that scholars should be
deprived for at least another twenty years of reaping the
benefits of any of our labors if we can make them accessible,
albeit in a limited and incomplete form. We have to balance
the needs of scholars against the complexities of our undertaking. I think our solution is the best, given all the circumstances.

II

But what of the pitfalls I have just mentioned? The problems of undertaking bibliographical research in Middle English
prose have not, to the best of my knowledge, ever received much
general consideration. It may be of value therefore to reflect
briefly on the range of difficulties that will confront us and
to suggest possible ways in which they may be resolved.

A number of questions arise, for instance, from our decision to make our *Index* a first-line index. The decision was
not, in itself, a difficult one to make. Our main aim is to
assist scholars seeking to record and identify prose texts,
generally in manuscript, and desiring relevant bibliographical
data about them. There seems to be no other method that will
afford more efficient access to that information.[6] But there
can often be difficulty in determining what properly constitutes the first line of a text. On occasion it is not possible
to distinguish with certainty between a preliminary rubric and
the actual beginning of a work. To take a typical example,
St. Brendan's Confession and Prayer as it appears in Lambeth
Palace 541 opens thus:

> Here bigynneþ a confessyoun which is also a preier
> þat Seynt Brandoun made, and it is riȝt needful to a
> Cristen man to seye and worche þer-after in his lyuynge.
>   I knowleche to þee, þou hiȝ increate and euerlastynge
> Trynyte þat is to seie, almiȝty God þe fadir, almiȝti
> God þe Sone....[7]

Which is the real first line? The sentence beginning "Here
bigynneþ ..." or the one which starts "I knowleche to þee ..."?
How do you tell? Initially, at the Handlist stage one would
doubtless include both with appropriate cross-references. In
the final *Index* it may be possible to decide whether one is

normative as the actual first line. But elsewhere it may never
be possible to provide a norm. Opening lines of the same work
can vary very markedly from copy to copy. Hilton's *Of Angel's
Song* begins in C.U.L. Dd.V.55:

> þow ȝernys perauenter gretely for to haue more knawynge
> & wyssynge þan þou has of aungels sange and heuenly
> sown qwat it is

But in the Thornton manuscript (Lincoln Cathedral 91) it
begins:

> Dere ffrende wit þou wele þat þe ende and þe soueraynte
> of perfeccione standes in a verray anehede of godde and
> of manes saule by perfyte charyte.

While in Henry Pepwell's 1521 edition it starts:

> Dere brother in Cryste I haue vnderstandynge by thyne
> owne speche and also by tellynge of another man þat þou
> yernest and desyrest gretely for to haue more knowledge
> and vnderstandynge then thou hast of aungelles songe.[8]

Such variation points up the need for caution, for avoiding an
uncritical trust in opening lines unsupported by other checks.
Our interim stage will prove of fundamental importance. Each
Handlist will include an elaborate system of cross-references
that will enable more precise identification of actual opening
lines and of variant openings to the same text. Thus all
opening rubrics, or seeming rubrics, will be recorded as well
as the apparent opening lines. We will include also the concluding lines of the text. In addition, in the case of longer
texts, the first lines of important subdivisions will be noted.
And for unidentified texts summaries will be given of their
contents. All first lines will be cumulated in each Handlist
(including a reverse index of concluding lines[9]) into a single
cumulative index. The effect should be to provide a comprehensive guide to the identification of prose works in a particular collection. When we begin to accumulate a series of
such guides for major collections we will have a clearer sense
of how much of this cross-reference will need to be retained
for the final *Index*. We hope that a large amount of it can
be eliminated in the finished work,[10] if it has shown up typical
forms for the openings of particular texts. We hope by being
exceptionally, indeed, excessively, detailed in the information
in our Handlists to thereby arrive at a more concise form for
the completed work.

This will resolve some, but by no means all, of the problems of a first-line index. There is, for instance, the question of macaronic works. Should they appear? If so, in what
form? Is it appropriate to treat such works as ordinary entries and insert them into an alphabetical Middle English
sequence? An indication of the nature of the problem may be
the beginning of the following sermon from Bodley 649, f. 128^v,
which begins:

> Supremus princeps celi et terre Deus qui creavit solum
> et mare pro socour humani generis rede us et cetera.
> Anglice: 'qwo sailet opoun þe see may ofte telle of
> perlys[11]

and which continues to regularly interweave Latin and English
throughout, usually within the same sentence. My own feeling
is that such works can be relegated to Appendices according
to the language other than English which is involved. Macaronic
text beginning in Middle English will be entered in the main
alphabetic sequence and cross-referenced to the relevant
Appendix. This will not solve all the difficulties presented
by macaronic works. There is, for instance, the difficulty
in determining whether a work has to have a minimum amount of
Middle English to qualify as properly macaronic. We will perhaps be well advised not to think too hard about this question
and to aim instead for a general inclusiveness in such Appendices even of texts containing only a minimal amount of Middle
English as they come under our purview,[12] while recognizing
that in the nature of things we may well miss a number. We
should not feel guilty about that.

A related difficulty is presented by texts which begin in
Latin (or another language), but are otherwise Middle English.
The Pepys manuscript of the *Ancrene Riwle* begins with forty-odd
words of Latin before breaking into English.[13] Other texts,
such as sermons or works like Rolle's *Ego Dormio*,[14] begin with
a Vulgate quotation. It may be appropriate simply to begin
indexing from the first word of the English where English and
the other language are so distinctly set off; an alternative--
probably superior--is the suggestion of Professor Lewis (see
below, pp. 46-47).

I labor these pedantic points because there are obvious
implications to a first-line index. All too rarely will it
be simply a case of straightforwardly transcribing opening
lines. Often there will be crucial questions to be resolved
before one can even perform the routine task of placing the
entry appropriately in an alphabetical sequence.

But the problems of determining the kind of index we should
produce pale in significance in comparison with the difficulties

of determining the subject matter of the *Index*. Our aim is to
index items in Middle English prose. But what is a Middle
English prose "item"? The question merits more than a moment's
reflection. The basic distinction between prose and verse
can, for instance, be a highly tenuous one. At least one
nineteenth-century editor actually printed a prose text as
verse.[15] One can only sympathize with his difficulties.[16]
The distinction between unrhymed alliterative prose and verse,
for example, is highly difficult to make at times.[17] Thus, to
pursue a formalist definition of what constitutes a prose work
is often not a very profitable exercise in Middle English.
To this difficulty must be added the fact that the ubiquity
of prose forces us to confront a staggering bulk of material
extending over a diverse range of purposes which have a
bearing on its form. Therefore, it has been necessary to ask
a pragmatic question: what classes of material is it likely to
prove impracticable to index at all, for whatever reasons?
Formulated in such a way, the question provides a basis for
exclusion from the *Index*, and hence the possibility of giving
it a manageable scope. The would-be user of the *Index* will
search in vain for a variety of materials. The great bulk of
excluded matter will be documentary in nature: deeds, statutes,
muniments, wills, inventories, petitions, assize and close
rolls, and the like. We also--and this I regret more--are
probably going to have to exclude all letters. I say this
with mixed feelings. The major collections--those of the
Pastons, Celys, and Stonors--are important documents in social
and literary history. But to include separate letters scattered through collections would simply prove impracticable.
As with the other excluded materials, the volume is very great.
And, like other documents, letters tend to have formulaic
openings which would render indexing of the kind we envisage
difficult if not impossible. For both letters and other classes
of excluded material calendaring is probably the most appropriate treatment.

There is, then, a bias in our work towards texts, however
short, and away from documents. This is, I fear, unavoidable
if our *Index* is to be practicable both in the time it takes to
complete and in its capability to offer its users intelligible
data through first-line retrieval. We will, however, attempt
to serve those whose interests we may appear to neglect by
recording (not indexing) the existence of documentary material
in the various Handlists of major collections. We can do no
less--and no more.

Our other main category of excluded material poses few
problems. We will be including virtually no dramatic materials
or records. The responsibility for all this has been shouldered
by the Records of Early English Drama (REED) project at the

University of Toronto. The *Index of Middle English Prose* is
in active collaboration with REED, whose Editor in Chief,
Alexandra Johnston, serves as a member of our Advisory Committee.

The omission of such blocks of material constitutes the
main attempt to reduce the scope of the *Index* to manageable
proportions. A few other types of prose will not normally be
included, such as lists, rubrics in English for works in other
languages, and brief jottings. These are all instances where
the slightness of the entry might make the task of indexing
wholly disproportionate to the significance of the material
recorded.

Such judgments involve a degree of subjectiveness and arbitrariness. E.A. Lowe, for example, has urged that "history
may lurk in every scribble."[18] We may, on occasion, simply
have to let it go on lurking. It may be better to aim for a
limited definitiveness than for a comprehensiveness that may
burden us all without significant compensating advantages.

This is not to say that setting up criteria for exclusion
of material is going to solve all our problems in determining
what constitutes a prose item. A moment ago I mentioned
macaronic works--texts where two languages are used in a single
work without any clear sense of their differentiation. But
there is also the problem of works written almost wholly in a
foreign language, but which, for various reasons, include
passages of significance in Middle English. One thinks, for
example, of Henry Knighton's *Chronicle*. This is a Latin
chronicle, but it contains several extended passages in Middle
English of interest to scholars of the Wycliffite movement.[19]
Similarly, in another Wycliffite work, the *Fasciculi Zizaniorum*,[20] parts of the account of the trial of the heretic John
Oldcastle--his declaration and various countervailing statements
of doctrine--appear in English rather than Latin. And the
enormously popular fourteenth-century religious compilation
the *Speculum Christiani*, although basically in Latin, does
possess a number of sections in English.[21] It seems likely
that in all these cases the decision to write or include
passages in English was a highly deliberate one, taken to
ensure the most effective communication of the material to the
widest possible audience. The general effect of such passages
is to give them the status of distinct works within larger ones.
Hence it requires no particular editorial anguish to decide
they must be included. But how far should the principle of
inclusion be extended in such cases?

To take another example--probably much more typical than
those I have just cited--Sloane 3744 contains, according to
its catalogue description, only texts in Latin. But in fact
there are several Middle English recipes scattered among these

texts.[22] Doubtless many other manuscripts contain similar
passages, more or less self-contained and brief, embedded in
the midst of otherwise foreign matter.

Such passages raise two related questions: what are the
criteria of inclusiveness and degree of comprehensiveness?
Within the material we have not already excluded, should there
be any minimum length stipulation? There may, in time, have
to be, but I would be reluctant to erect arbitrary criteria
based on number of words or lines. It may prove in the long
run less arbitrary to include any passage, however brief, that
makes a coherent statement. One might therefore include some
isolated brief passages, such as (say) charms, or proverbs,
but not include, for instance, somewhat longer passages of
comparable length but less importance, such as chapter headings.[23] I am conscious of treading on dangerous ground here,
offering imprecision at just the point where some may feel it
vital that there be exactitude. I confess to being unrepentant.
We cannot strain overmuch after gnats given the number of very
healthy-sized camels that confront us.

The question of comprehensiveness in our searching for
materials is also relevant here. The recipes in Sloane 3744
came to light by chance. But it seems, as I have said, to be
a typical case. Is it therefore to be incumbent on every
scholar to turn over every leaf of every manuscript in the
collection he happens to be examining? It may indeed be
necessary to do this for some collections (such as Longleat)
where no catalogue exists at all. But for many major collections there are catalogues that can at least indicate what
manuscripts contain Middle English prose even if not the actual
prose they contain. Wherever possible we will, I feel, have
to rely on existing catalogues unless there are clear reasons
for denying their reliability. It is not necessarily reasonable
to expect a scholar to undertake leaf-by-leaf examinations of
every manuscript in "his" collection. The effort involved may
be wholly disproportionate to the end result in terms of
identifying new material of significance. This may well lead
to the omission of some brief items that ought to be included.
I accept this as inevitable--even necessary if we wish to avoid
adding fruitless years to our task.

To illustrate my point: the Lambeth Palace Library contains
(roughly) six hundred medieval manuscripts. Of these, about
sixty contain Middle English prose.[24] It might take an experienced scholar, working fulltime, perhaps three months to
examine and compile draft entries for the relevant material in
those sixty manuscripts. What then? Should he pass on to the
other ninety percent of the collection, the mere initial examination of which will probably occupy him for the better
part of a year? Or should he move on in quest of other manu-

scripts which certainly do contain relevant material? I would
urge the latter course, given that all of those involved in
this project will have limited opportunities (and limited
energies) to devote to their task. If we leave some small
work for future generations, that is perhaps as it should be.

My response to these difficulties may seem (indeed be)
cavalier, arbitrary, and unmethodical. I would prefer, however, to see it as pragmatic, given the scope and complexity
of our undertaking. There may be a certain very restricted
incompleteness in coverage in the completed work. Rather than
wring our hands over this it may be better to concentrate on
the difficulties we are likely to encounter with the material
we *do* find and *do* decide to include.

It may not always be possible, even given what we have
already excluded, to treat our material in as detailed a manner as we might wish. I mentioned recipes a moment ago.
Should we aim to index every separate recipe in every collection? Or can groups of recipes be treated as single entities?
There may be problems in adopting the latter course.[25] But
including every recipe, even in the Handlists, will prove a
very burdensome business. Similarly, in the case of sermon
cycles, indexing a single manuscript may yield hundreds of
entries. A number of questions arise, not the least of which
is: would any publisher stand for this? One possible solution
may be to remove all this detailed indexing from the *Index*
proper and have supplementary bibliographical catalogues of
the kind I have already mentioned dealing with sermons and
recipes, which will allow a more summary treatment in the
Index proper. This may seem laborious and overly circuitous--
supplementing one *Index* with further indices--but it may prove
an inevitable solution.

Our difficulties will not be confined to such generically
coherent, but not necessarily unified, sequences of material
as sermons and recipes. Often we will find ourselves confronted
with the problem of determining whether a work is in fact *a*
work or several. Indeed, this may not always be possible.
Peter Jolliffe observes of one set of tracts that "it has
proved impossible to separate one from another with certainty."[26] These difficulties can be considerable. It would be
nice if others had evinced a similar degree of caution. As it
is, we will have to avoid several bibliographical traps laid
down by fellow scholars. I leave aside the question of what
one should do with Malory's *Le Morte Arthur*. Or should it be
The Works of Sir Thomas Malory?[27] One work, or eight? Others
have been equally eager to see disunity where it does not
exist. One scholar "discovered" a separate tract on the Maundy
Thursday and Easter Saturday rituals in a manuscript of the
homiletic collection Mirk's *Festial*.[28] But, in fact, this

"tract" is part of the normal cycle of *Festial* homilies and
the scholar seems to have been misled by its separate appearance in a single manuscript.[29] And even as reliable a guide
as Jolliffe occasionally classifies as separate tracts works
which seem actually to be divisions of a single work.[30] Such
instances point up the need for tact and caution in the preparation of entries. Especially at the Handlist stage we will
have a great deal of cross-referencing and quotation of opening
lines of separate divisions of a work, in the hope that we can
thereby gradually build up a picture of the real nature and
contents of particular texts.

    This brings up a related, even larger, problem: the problem
of manuscript selections from larger works, quite often without
explicit identification of the original. The list of examples
is huge: there was an inevitable tendency to fragment longer
texts with no sense of their larger unity. In some manuscripts
of Hilton's *Scale of Perfection*, both books appear as separate
entities, divorced by other matter.[31] Short texts such as
Rolle's *Form of Living* can appear in a remarkable variety of
extracted forms.[32] Elsewhere, parts of larger texts seem to
have established their own separate identity. The final chapter of the pseudo-Rolle *Contemplations of the Dread and Love
of God* occurs separately in four manuscripts without any
reference to the larger work.[33] Two chapters from *The Chastising of God's Children* appear extracted in a Harley manuscript.[34] The anonymous *Formula Noviciorum* seems to have been
regularly excerpted.[35] A new text of part of Trevisa's *Gospel
of Nichodemus* has only recently come to light, joined to a
non-Trevisan rendering.[36] Parts of his *Polychronicon* are extracted in at least two manuscripts.[37] These rather random
examples indicate the scope of the problem. They point up the
need to be sensitive to the widespread borrowing by one work
from another. When preparing entries we will have to be constantly alert to the likelihood that a particular item is not
what it seems, that a seeming acquaintance is possibly a
thinly disguised old friend--or part of one. It is only
through this laborious process of identification that we will
come to an adequate understanding of the circulation, reputa-
tion, and influence of certain texts.

    There are related types of modification to separate texts
which pose equally challenging problems. One obvious one is
conflated texts which cannibalize existing material and weld
it into new forms. One thinks, for example, of the *Disce Mori*,
which includes without acknowledgment parts of Hilton's *Eight
Chapters of Perfection*, almost half the text of *The Chastising
of God's Children*, part of Rolle's *Emendatio Vitae* in an
English translation, together with other tracts which elsewhere
appear separately.[38] The "Treatise of Ghostly Battle" (extant

in at least nine manuscripts) is cobbled together out of
various other works, including bits from the *Pore Caytyf* and
the pseudo-Rolle "Three Arrows of Doomsday."[39]   Huntington
MS HM 145, ff. 1-22[v] is a pastiche of passages from separate
treatises of Rolle and his followers.[40]   An interesting secular
illustration is Hunterian MS T.3.21 of the late fifteenth century, which conflates various versions of the *Brut* with Caxton's continuation of the *Polychronicon* and a copy of Warkworth's *Chronicle*. This last is of particular interest because
until it was recently identified, Warkworth's *Chronicle* had
been known to exist in only a single manuscript.[41]   It is
likely that sustained examination of particular unpublished
texts is going to reveal many comparable instances of conflated
material and consequently increase the numbers of particular
works. It is clearly going to be our duty to untangle the
various strands of compilation in works of this kind. It
follows that many entries are going to require a considerable
amount of time and effort to complete. Once again, the benefit
of our Handlist stage will be clear. It will afford us an
opportunity to catch any missed identifications prior to the
preparation of the final *Index*.
     I have said enough to suggest some of the more obvious
implications of our attempts to deal with prose "items." But
I have so far avoided one equally crucial question: *when* was
Middle English prose? The question of cutoff dates must inevitably loom large in our thinking, for we lack objective
criteria to assist us in determining them. We do plan to
assume that Middle English begins *circa* 1200. Some scholars
would hold that it begins somewhat earlier.[42]   But sooner than
involve ourselves in heated linguistic controversy, we will,
once again, aim at a pragmatic resolution to the question.
Neil Ker's *Catalogue of Manuscripts Containing Anglo Saxon*
(Oxford, 1957) stops *circa* 1200, and it is appropriate that
our labors begin where his leave off in respect of vernacular
texts. Such a starting point may seem arbitrary, as believers
in the continuity of English prose may be quick to point out,
but it is as reasonable as any necessarily rough-and-ready
decision can be. There may be slight problems of overlapping
nonetheless. An example is Blickling Hall 6864 (now in the
Scheide Library, Princeton), which contains a copy of the
Creed at the end of the final quire. Dr. Ker excluded it from
his original *Catalogue* on codicological grounds. But recently
he changed his mind and decided that palaeographically it
belongs within his period.[43]   I find the decision a debatable
one--the codicological argument perhaps has a little more
force than the palaeographical. But the evidence is in no
sense clear-cut and I am prepared to abandon it to Dr. Ker--
for the present at least. But I cite the example simply to

indicate the difficulty in making clear-cut decisions.

There are far greater difficulties with our terminal date
of *circa* 1500. Professor Robbins' experience with the *Index
of Middle English Verse* requires that such a date not be en-
forced with any rigor.[44] Chronicles, to give an obvious instance, often cut across such divisions. A number of Middle
English works survive solely in sixteenth-century manuscripts.[45]
Still others appear uniquely in early printed editions; an
obvious example is Usk's *Testament of Love*, known only from
the 1532 edition of Chaucer. In certain cases all the authorities for a text postdate our *terminus ad quem*. A notable
illustration is the long version of Julian of Norwich's *Revelations*, which survives in only one pre-Dissolution witness
and that an early sixteenth-century selected text. The main
authorities are all later--and include a printed edition of
1670.[46] Our contributors are going to face the burden of
attempting to uncover and identify such post-1500 copies in
addition to their other tasks. Clearly our search for material
is going to require considerable flexibility and a willingness
to extend inquiry beyond the immediately and obviously medieval
materials they encounter.[47] And often it will be impossible
to resolve whether a work or manuscript is "*circa* 1500" or
"early sixteenth century." We will have inevitably to aim for
a generous inclusiveness when confronted with such difficulties. Rigidity in enforcing of dates will prove impossible.

                              III

I think I have said enough--indeed, probably too much--to
make clear the reasons for my choice of title. I have tried
to suggest some of the major difficulties confronting us as
we plan the preparation of the *Index of Middle English Prose*
which are not susceptible to clear-cut or rigid solutions.
The preparation of individual entries is therefore of necessity
going to be a slow and taxing business calling for skills of
a diversity and depth not invariably required of bibliographers.
The need for such qualities has governed our selection of
Contributing Editors, on whom the initial burden of much of
the work will fall as they prepare the Handlists of major
collections. There will ultimately be from fifty to one hundred such scholars, all chosen for their experience and competence within the field. One can only be grateful to so many
scholars who have been prepared to undertake a task whose
demands are likely to far outweigh any possible rewards. And
yet, as I have tried to indicate, the work is not of a kind
that could be undertaken by other than experienced scholars
with any certainty that it would be executed with the standard
of competence we require.

What we are contemplating is an enormous bibliographical
undertaking arguably surpassing in scope and complexity even
the great achievements of our age--the *Short Title Catalogue*,
Wing, Foxon, the *Index of Middle English Verse*. And whereas
these achievements have tended to be the work of one or two
dedicated scholars, our work will require a high degree of
international collaboration if we are to bring it to completion even within two decades. Our material is too great and
too scattered for it to be otherwise. It is to be found not
only in the obvious institutional libraries of Great Britain,
North America, and Europe, but in places as far afield as
Australia and Japan. Some probably still lurks unnoticed in
record repositories. And there is an increasing number of
manuscripts passing through the sale room into private collections. It is going to require much labor, patience, and
tact--and much good fortune--to trace and examine this material
--especially as we wait nervously for the next transfusion
into the manuscript market from the Bibliotheca Phillippica.
    Yet the potential rewards are enormous. Recent genera-
tions of medievalists have witnessed the rediscovery of such
treasures of Middle English prose as the manuscripts of Malory,
Marjory Kempe, and *The Equatorie of the Planets*. Doubtless,
discoveries of comparable magnitude will fall to our lot.
Clearly our project has profound implications for many aspects
of medieval studies. It is quite possible that standard
accounts of history and literature, of science and religion,
in the medieval period will have to be rewritten in the light
of our work. The road ahead is a long and arduous one, strewn
with frustrations and adversities. We may not all live to
see the consummation of our labors. But let us sustain ourselves with a vision of the lasting benefit to scholarship
that our efforts will bring.[48]

                                        A.S.G. Edwards
                                        University of Victoria

NOTES

    1. In, for example, a review article in *Speculum*, 32
(1957), 406-10; in the *Supplement to the Index of Middle
English Verse* (Lexington, Ky., 1965), p. xxiv; and (most extensively) in "Mirth in Manuscripts," *Essays & Studies*, n.s.
21 (1968), 1-28.

    2. *A Check-List of Middle English Prose Writings of
Spiritual Guidance* (Toronto, 1974), probably the most useful
work on the subject published to date.

3. The revision of J.E. Wells' original *Manual* began in the early 1950s under the auspices of the Modern Language Association. So far, five volumes have appeared, few of which deal with with Middle English prose, and those not with uniform success. See, for example, Anne Hudson, "Contributions to a Bibliography of Wycliffite Writings," *Notes & Queries*, 218 (1973), 443-53, which examines some of the lacunae in the account in the revised *Manual*.

4. *Fifteenth Century English Prayers and Meditations* (New York, 1975).

5. Jolliffe, for example, found it impossible to include some items within single categories and had to include them twice; see (for example) items C.10 and O.12, M.5 and O.15, F.10 and O.16, M.1 and O.2.

6. Jolliffe discusses the use of *incipits* for indexing Middle English prose (pp. 34-36) and concludes: "It provides the most satisfactory record of the facts which it is possible to achieve without committing the writer to an interpretation of them" (p. 36). He does not, however, discuss the distinction between introductory formulae and the beginning of the text proper.

7. See "The Middle English *St. Brendan's Confession and Prayer*," edited by Fumio Kuriyagawa in *Geibun-Kenkyu* (Tokyo), 25 (1968), 5.

8. All three versions are conveniently printed in C. Horstman, ed., *Yorkshire Writers*, 2 vols. (1895-96), I, 175.

9. Such a reverse index would show up, for instance, the relationship between the variant texts of Hilton's *Of Angel's Song* since they end in the same form. It will also be of obvious value in identifying acephalous texts.

10. Most probably the reverse index of concluding lines would not, for example, be included.

11. Cited in R.M. Haines, "'Our Master Mariner, Our Sovereign Lord': A Contemporary Preacher's View of King Henry V," *Mediaeval Studies*, 38 (1976), 87-88.

12. For examples of such texts (which are countless) see a philosophical text in Pavia MS 69, edited by S.H. Thomson in *Modern Language Notes*, 49 (1934), 237; the exempla from Oxf. Magdalen 60 and Advocates' 18.4.4 printed by Mary E. Barnicle in *PMLA*, 33 (1918), 415-16, 417-18; and the sermon printed by A.G. Little in *Franciscan Papers Lists and Documents* (Manchester, 1943), pp. 247-56, from Bodl. Lat. Th. D.i.

13. See *The English Text of the Ancrene Riwle edited from Magdalene College, Cambridge MS. Pepys 2498*, ed. A. Zettersten, EETS, o.s. 274 (London, 1976), p. 1, lines 1-6.

14. Rolle's work begins: "*Ego dormio et cor meum vigilat.* þai þat lyste lufe, herken, and here of luf." *English Writings of Richard Rolle*, ed. H.E. Allen (Oxford, 1931), p. 61.

15. See *The Legend of St. Katherine of Alexandria*, ed. James Morton, Abbotsford Club (1841). Morton describes this work (in B.L. Cotton Titus D.xviii) as a "poetic Legend" (ix); it is in alliterative prose.

16. For a full bibliography of the controversy as to whether *St. Katherine* is in verse or prose, see J. Burke Severs, ed., *A Manual of the Writings in Middle English*, 2 (New Haven, 1970), 599-600.

17. For a general discussion of the problems of distinguishing verse from prose see *Middle English Religious Prose*, ed. N.F. Blake (London, 1972), pp. 6-8; see also E. Salter, "Alliterative Modes and Affiliations in the Fourteenth Century," *Neuphilologische Mitteilungen*, 79 (1978), 25-35.

18. *Codices latini antiquiores*, 6 (Oxford, 1963), ix.

19. *Chronicon Henrici Knighton*, ed. J.R. Lumby, Rolls Series 92 (1895). The passages I have in mind appear on pp. 138-40, 161-62, 170-72 of Volume II. One of these passages at least (that on pp. 161-62) had a separate existence in manuscript. It appears separately in Bodley 647; see further *Select English Works of John Wyclif*, ed. T. Arnold (1869-1871), III, 502-503.

20. See Thomas Netter, *Fasciculi Zizaniorum Magistri Johannis Wyclif*, ed. W.W. Shirley, Rolls Series 5 (1858). The relevant passages appear on pp. 438-39, 441-42. Neither of these passages appears to be noted in the account of Middle English Wycliffite writings in J. Burke Severs, ed., *A Manual of the Writings in Middle English*, 2 (New Haven, 1970), 517-33.

21. See *Speculum Christiani*, ed. G. Holmstedt, EETS, o.s. 182 (London, 1933), pp. 75-82, 83-87, 87-101, 103-19 (odd pages only).

22. I am indebted to Professor Roger Dahood for drawing my attention to these recipes.

23. I am thinking of such passages as the chapter summaries to the verse romance *Titus and Vespasian*; they are printed by C.F. Bühler, "The New Morgan Manuscript of *Titus and Vespasian*," *PMLA*, 76 (1961), 21.

24. M.R. James, *A Descriptive Catalogue of the Manuscripts in the Library of Lambeth Palace: The Mediaeval Manuscripts* (Cambridge, 1932); see also E.W.G. Bill, *A Catalogue of Manuscripts in Lambeth Palace Library: MSS. 1222-1860* (Oxford, 1972). My figures are based on these catalogues.

25. I draw here on Dr. Henry Hargreaves' "Some Problems in Indexing Middle English Recipes," see below, pp. 91-113.

26. Jolliffe, p. 83 (F.17).

27. This is the title given to the unique Winchester manuscript by its editor, Eugène Vinaver. The majority of scholars has found his characterization unacceptable and prefer to see the manuscript as a single work.

28. Karl Young, "Instructions for Parish Priests," *Speculum*, 11 (1936), 224-31.

29. See M.F. Wakelin, "The Manuscripts of John Mirk's Festial," *Leeds Studies in English*, n.s. 1 (1967), 97-98. The manuscript in question is B.L. Harley 2250.

30. See, for example, items D.8 and D.13 in his *Checklist*.

31. See S.S. Hussey, "The Text of *The Scale of Perfection*, Book II," *Neuphilologische Mitteilungen*, 65 (1964), 77.

32. For details see H.E. Allen, *Writings Ascribed to Richard Rolle* (New York, 1927), for example, pp. 260-61, 274, 359; and *Yorkshire Writers*, I, 106, 136, 196-97, 412-15, for illustrations of each selection. A reworked text based on passages from the *Form* appears in *Yorkshire Writers*, I, 416-20.

33. See J.E. Krochalis, "*Contemplations of the Dread and Love of God*: Two Newly Identified Pennsylvania Manuscripts," *The Library Chronicle*, 42 (1977), 9-10.

34. Harley 1288, ff. 81^v-86^v contains chapters xxiv-xxv; see *The Chastising of God's Children*, ed. J. Bazire and E. Colledge (Oxford, 1957), p. 5.

35. See Jolliffe, p. 91, H.2.

36. See Kathleen H. Power, "A Newly Identified Prose Version of the Trevisa Version of the Gospel of Nicodemus," *Notes & Queries*, 223 (1978), 5-7.

37. See A.S.G. Edwards, "A Sixteenth Century Version of Trevisa's *Polychronicon*," *English Language Notes*, 11 (1973), 34-38, for details. A further version appears in Rawlinson C. 86. I am indebted to Dr. Christina von Nolcken and Professor Derek Pearsall for this information.

38. See Anne Hudson, "A Chapter from Walter Hilton in Two Middle English Compilations," *Neophilologus*, 52 (1968), 416-21; Allen, *English Writings*, p. 243; *The Chastising of God's Children*, p. 6; and Jolliffe, I.35(b) and K.1. Other such compilations include the enormously popular *Pore Caytyf* and the *Ignorancia Sacerdotum*.

39. The text is edited in *Yorkshire Writers*, II, 420-36; for bibliography see Jolliffe, p. 92 (H.3).

40. I owe this information to Professor Ralph Hanna.

41. I am indebted to Dr. Lister Matheson for the information; see the summary account of his findings in *Manuscripta*, 22 (1978), 15-16.

42. For details see Kemp Malone, "When Did Middle English Begin," in *Curme Volume of Linguistic Studies* (*Language* Monographs 7, 1930), 110-17.

43. "A Supplement to 'Catalogue of Manuscripts Containing Anglo-Saxon,'" *Anglo Saxon England*, 5 (1976), 126-27; the copy of the Creed was edited by A.S. Napier in *Modern Language Notes*, 4 (1889), 138. In his original *Catalogue* (xix) Ker points out the difficulty of distinguishing clearly between Old and Middle English.

44. See his comments in the *Supplement to the Index of Middle English Verse*, pp. xiv-xvi.

45. Some of these are conveniently listed by Jolliffe, pp. 24-25; see also Hudson, "Contributions ...," p. 450 for some Wycliffite examples.

46. For details see E. Colledge and J. Walsh, "Editing Julian of Norwich's *Revelations*: A Progress Report," *Mediaeval Studies*, 38 (1976), 404-27.

47. It is also worth reflecting that our search for materials will not be restricted to such obvious forms as manuscripts and printed books. It will also have to encompass (for example) rolls and possibly even in some cases inscriptions.

48. For helpful commentary on an earlier draft of this paper I am indebted to Dr. A.I. Doyle, Professors Derek Pearsall and R.E. Lewis, and Mr. R.A. Waldron. I am, of course, solely responsible for both opinions and errors.

EDITORIAL TECHNIQUE IN THE
INDEX OF MIDDLE ENGLISH PROSE

In theory, there are at least five possible ways, deriving from the material itself, in which Middle English prose can be indexed--by author, by title, by date of composition, by genre, and by first line--and all of these ways have been used before, either separately or in combination, but I am going to assume at the outset that all would agree that the best way is by first line.[1] First of all, it is more comprehensive and more precise than any of the other ways. Indexing by author and indexing by title can immediately be eliminated as not all-inclusive: most Middle English prose has no known author, and it would not be very enlightening to have "Anon." as the main entry for three-quarters of an index; much Middle English prose is without title as well, and it would not be much better to have an index a large portion of which would have the entry "Without Title." The third way, indexing by date of composition, *is* all-inclusive, but the date of composition is simply speculation for most Middle English prose, and any index based on that would be subject to constant revision and argument. The fourth way, indexing by genre, is also all-inclusive, but generic distinctions are notoriously imprecise and subjective, probably more so with prose than with verse if one can judge from two recent books that attempt to classify parts of our subject by genre, Peter Jolliffe's *Check-List of Middle English Prose Writings of Spiritual Guidance* (1974) and Peter Revell's *Fifteenth Century English Prayers and Meditations* (1975).

Secondly, the majority of similar reference tools and indexes used in medieval studies are organized by first line. Here Carleton Brown and Rossell Hope Robbins' *Index of Middle English Verse* (1943; hereafter *IMEV*) must surely take pride of place; both it and the *Supplement* (1965) by Robbins and John L. Cutler, as well as the second volume of its predecessor, Carleton Brown's *Register of Middle English Religious and Didactic Verse* (1920), are first-line indexes, alphabetically arranged. And there are many others, such as Margaret Crum's *First-Line Index of English Poetry, 1500-1800* (1969), or

Francis L. Utley's *Crooked Rib* (1944), or Morton Bloomfield's
"List of Incipits of Latin Works on the Virtues and Vices"
(*Traditio*, 11 [1955]), or A.G. Little's *Initia Operum Latin-
orum* (1904), or Lynn Thorndike and Pearl Kibre's *Catalogue of
Incipits of Mediaeval Scientific Writings in Latin* (revised
ed. 1963), to name only some of the best-known ones. And of
course most indexes, even when they are organized in another
way, have an index of first lines--D.F. Foxon's *English Verse,
1701-1750* (1975), for example, or the books by Jolliffe and
Revell.

So I begin with the assumption that both the *Index of
Middle English Prose in Print 1476-1976* (Stage 1 of the
project; hereafter *IMEP in Print*) and the final *Index of
Middle English Prose* (Stage 3 of the project; hereafter *IMEP*)
will be first-line indexes, arranged alphabetically, on the
model of *IMEV*.[2] But a first-line index is only as good as
its indices and appendices, and it is essential for these, as
well as the cross-references, to be as full and as useful as
possible. The greatest drawback of *IMEV* as a research tool
is that it has no list of the manuscripts cited in the body
of the work.[3] Such a list is not a luxury: it is absolutely
indispensable if one wants to discover what other Middle
English works appear in a particular manuscript or what com-
pany a particular work keeps in manuscript. It is so important
that we will even include one in *IMEP in Print*. The other
essential information--that is, authors, titles, genres, subjects, and so forth--can perhaps be handled in one general
index in *IMEP in Print*, but given the enormous amount of such
information in *IMEP*, it will doubtless be necessary to have
separate indices for each important area of information.

I would like now to state a few general principles of
format for *IMEP*--principles that represent a consensus reached
by Professors Blake and Edwards and myself for *IMEP in Print*
but that for *IMEP*, which is years away, represent my own preliminary and tentative thinking. I will speak in the first
person throughout so as not to implicate my colleagues in
decisions that they and others might find unreasonable. I
will also try to stick to broad general principles, though inevitably minor and specific details will enter into the discussion. I will illustrate these general principles as I go
along from the examples in the Appendix, especially the first
two, which are relatively straightforward (the first is the
entry for *Hali Meidenhad* in *IMEP in Print*, the second the
same entry for *IMEP*).

First, the first line. There was no problem with this in
IMEV: if the poem was in rhyming couplets, the first two lines
were given; if the poem was in alliterative verse, the first
line was given. For *IMEP* we do not have that convenience,

and so the question is how many words to print. For the Handlists of individual collections (Stage 2 of the project), the
number will be at least fifty, but the Handlists serve a purpose different from that of the two comprehensive Indexes, and
I think fifty is more than we need, and more than we can ask
a publisher to print. As a general rule I have settled on
twenty to thirty, which for most texts is enough to give a
sense of the beginning and to produce a line that can stand
on its own syntactically, though occasionally I have fewer
(items 4, 16, and 19). In transcribing the first line
for both Indexes I have omitted all punctuation but have retained capital letters. For entries in *IMEP in Print* I have
reproduced the words of the line exactly as they appear in the
printed edition, but I have not reproduced italicized suspen-
sions, superscript marks and letters, abbreviations that would
not appear in the typeface to be used for the actual printing,[4]
and the like. For entries in *IMEP* I have reproduced the line
exactly as it appears in the manuscript or incunabulum, with
abbreviations silently expanded if there was no question about
their expansion.

The first line will be the first line of the actual Middle
English text--omitting titles, tables of contents, and prefatory material--which sounds easy in theory but is often difficult in practice. For example, I have omitted the prefatory
material (nine lines) for item 6 because it gives the title,
tells why the work has been translated into English, and ex-
plains for what audience the translation has been made, but
for item 19 I have kept the prefatory material and have taken
the first line from it because, though it does give the title,
as in item 6, it goes on to say what the treatise is about.
This may not seem an entirely convincing distinction, and it
may be possible to refine it as we go along, but finally, I
think, one must simply exercise one's best judgment in cases
like these. It is important, however, always to note when the
prefatory material has been omitted, as I have done at the
end of the entry for the first printed edition in item 6.

What does one do if a Middle English prose text begins
with words in a foreign language? One might argue that because
we are making an *Index* of *English* prose, we should begin with
the English text. I think that argument has flaws. *Hali
Meidenhad* (items 1 and 2) and the *Ancrene Riwle* (items 13 and
14) are Middle English prose works that happen to begin with
Latin quotations from the Old Testament, and it would be mis-
representing their first lines to ignore those quotations.
One solution would be to give the Latin first line but then to
alphabetize the entry under the first word of English. I
would prefer to do what *IMEV* does: to give the Latin first
line and to alphabetize the entry under the first word of

Latin. On the other hand, it is important to get the first
words of English into a first line, but to do so for, say, the
Ancrene Riwle would mean having an entry of over fifty words,
since there are forty-three words of Latin at the beginning.
My compromise solution is to give enough of the Latin to make
it free-standing but then to omit the rest (indicated by three
dots) and go right on to the first words of the English. I
have, however (unlike *IMEV*), as an additional aid to the reader, listed the first few words of the English as a separate
but unnumbered entry with a cross-reference to the main entry.

The first line should be taken from the first listed edition in *IMEP in Print* or the first listed manuscript or incunabulum for *IMEP*, as in items 6, 9, and 19, unless there is
good reason not to. In the case of *Hali Meidenhad*, Bodley 34
is the older of the two manuscripts and in the AB dialect and
therefore presumably closer to the original; so I believe the
first line should be taken from it. I have indicated in
parentheses after the first line where it comes from. An
alternative to this would be to elevate the edition or manuscript from which the first line is taken to the head of the
list, but I prefer doing it for *IMEP in Print* as I have done
in item 1 because, in addition to everything else, we want
to illustrate the printing history of a work and doing it for
IMEP as I have done in item 2 because there will be less chance
for a reader to overlook the first manuscript later on in his
work.

The actual indexing of the first lines should be alphabetical, as I am sure all would agree, though, given the
enormous amount of material that will be in *IMEP*, I would
hesitate to put articles into the alphabetical scheme, as
IMEV does. Each individual entry should have a number; cross-
references (whether first lines or key words) should not.
Variant spellings of initial words should be grouped together,
as in *IMEV*, with appropriate cross-references where necessary;
it is frustrating to use, for example, M.J. Preston's *Concordance to the Middle English Shorter Poem* (1975) and to
have to think of every possible variant spelling of a word
in order to locate all occurrences of it.[5] Unidentifiable
acephalous items should go into the alphabetical scheme, as
in the *Supplement* to *IMEV*, and we might also consider doing
what Margaret Crum does in her *First-Line Index of English
Poetry, 1500-1800*--that is, listing the final words as well
as the first--as an aid to the reader interested in trying
to identify an unknown item. On the other hand, known works
beginning imperfectly and fragments from known works should
not have their first lines listed.

The most difficult question for me concerning the actual
indexing is whether to list *all* first lines of texts that

appear in multiple manuscripts. If the first lines differ by
an insignificant word or two, as the first line of the Nero
manuscript of the *Ancrene Riwle* does (by a relative particle
and a relative pronoun) from the first line in item 14, one
should certainly not list them both: it serves no useful purpose (giving no clue to textual affiliations), and moreover
is a waste of space. But what about lines that differ substantively (by "substantively" I mean in additions, substitu-
tions, and most omissions of nouns, verbs, adjectives, and
adverbs)? Here there is no perfect solution, and each case
would need to be decided individually, but my rule of thumb
would be that if one first line differs substantively from
another of the same text in the first five or ten words, I
would list it as a separate but unnumbered entry and would
give a cross-reference to the main entry; doing this would
be especially important if the difference or differences put
the first line in another part of the *Index* or if they coincide with a difference in the textual affiliations of the two
manuscripts having the first lines. On the other hand, I
would not give the first line a separate entry if the substantive change is farther down the line,[6] if it is only in one
word (perhaps a synonym or an omission),[7] and if it follows
the main entry alphabetically in the *Index*. For example, in
the Pepys manuscript of the *Ancrene Riwle*, the words that immediately follow the first line in item 14--"[And ʒe] mine
leove sustren habbeð moni dei icraved on me efter riwle"--
are omitted, and though the omission is interesting because
it shows the Pepys scribe adapting the text to a different
audience, in terms of the complete text it is sixty-three
words down the line. I would therefore not list it. A first-
line index can do only so much: it is not capable of providing
a complete guide to the textual affiliations of the manuscripts
of a work.

The other items in the entry call for less comment than
the first line. The second section of the entry should include the following information, in order: author, title,
genre, and date of composition. First, the author. My practice has been to give the author's name without comment when
it is clear who he is (as in item 9), to put a question mark
after the author's name when it is probable but not absolutely
certain who he is (as in item 17), to put square brackets
around the author's name when a work has been attributed to
him but it is highly unlikely that he wrote it (no example in
the Appendix, but *Contemplations of the Dread and Love of God*
would be one, for which "[Attrib. to Rolle]" would appear
first), and simply to make no comment when a work is anonymous
(as in items 1 and 2): to do otherwise would fill the *Index*
unnecessarily with "Anon."

The second item is the title. I have given the title as
it appears in manuscript or incunabulum, with spelling nor-
malized, when this is the title by which the work is known
(as in items 17 and 19). If that title has no manuscript
authority (as in items 1, 2, 9, 13, and 14), I have put it
in square brackets, with any titles *with* manuscript authority
in parentheses after it (as in items 1, 9, 13, and 14). When
a work has no title whatsoever, I have simply gone on to
the generic description (no examples in the Appendix, but
most sermons would fall into this category). My practice differs in the two Indexes: e.g., in item 1, the *Hali Meidenhad*
entry for *IMEP in Print*, I have put the titles *Hali Meidenhad*
and *Hali Meiðhad* first because they are the ones by which the
treatise is known in print, followed by the title in Bodley
34, *Epistel of Meidenhad*, which does have manuscript authority
but is virtually unknown; on the other hand, *IMEP* will be a
manuscript and incunabulum index, and for the *Hali Meidenhad*
entry there (item 2) I have given the manuscript title first,
but with the two better-known titles in square brackets following. One might consider this information superfluous, but
I think the reader needs it for ease of identification. Compare, however, the two entries for the *Ancrene Riwle* (items
13 and 14): as with *Hali Meidenhad*, the title by which the
work is usually known appears first in the entry for *IMEP in
Print* (item 13), in square brackets because it is unattested
in manuscript, with those titles with manuscript authority
in parentheses following. For *IMEP* (item 14) I have not re-
versed the items as I did in the *Hali Meidenhad* entry. I was
tempted to use *Ancrene Wisse* from the revised version in the
Corpus manuscript as the main title, as E.J. Dobson and others
do, but it is not certain that the original title *was Ancrene
Wisse*, since the word *riwle* is used so often in the introduction to the work. Thus my solution.
        The third item is genre. Generic distinctions are always
difficult to make, especially in a few words, but my own opinion about this category is that we should strive to give the
reader a brief hint about the nature of a work rather than to
fit that work into a predetermined and fixed generic classification. For *Hali Meidenhad* I have been brief: "homiletic
treatise," so far as I can tell from the scholarship, represents informed opinion on the matter. For items 4, 5, and 6
I have added information that I thought would be useful to the
reader. In item 9 the title indicates the genre, and a further
description would be superfluous. The *Ancrene Riwle* (items 13
and 14) is not a rule in the sense in which the Benedictine
Rule is a rule, and I have called it simply a "guide for nuns."
The genre of item 17 is self-evident from the title, and I
have omitted a generic description; the genre of item 19 is

not self-evident, and I have given it a rather lengthy description, including the information that it is a translation from French. In both cases I have indicated the dependence on parts of the *Ancrene Riwle*, which is the kind of useful information we should include if it is easily available.

The last item is date of composition, and here I have simply followed informed opinion on the matter. For the *Ancrene Riwle* I have added Dobson's more precise dating in parentheses: this is not absolutely necessary, but it is the latest opinion, and I see no reason not to include such information if it is easily available.[8]

The third section of the entry will contain, for *IMEP in Print*, a numbered listing, arranged chronologically, of all editions of the complete work.[9] In item 1, for example, the first printed edition is Cockayne's for the EETS, with the base manuscript and folio numbers in parentheses following (for series like this and for journals it seems unnecessary to give either the editor's name or the actual title of the book or article). Item 2 is Furnivall's re-edition, which adds Bodley 34, the earlier manuscript: note that on the second occurrence of a base manuscript, both here and elsewhere in the examples in the Appendix, I refer to the first for the necessary information about both the manuscript and the nature of the text in it. Regarding item 3 in the entry, my policy is to give the title of the edition before the editor's name if it is also the title of the work; compare this with item 5 in the same entry, where I give the editor's name first because the book title has no mention of *Hali Meidenhad*. In this entry, and in the others, I have tried to be as brief as possible but also to give the reader enough bibliographical information so that he will be able to find the edition in a library.[10] In all cases I have given the date of the edition, both because it helps the reader locate the edition, especially in series and journals, and because it illustrates the printing history of a work. Item 4 in the entry, EETS, o.s. 247, is a facsimile of Bodley 34, but because it is in fact a printed edition, it should be listed.

The third section of the entry for *IMEP* will contain a numbered listing of all manuscripts and, where appropriate (as in items 6 and 19), printed editions, arranged alphabetically by city, library, collection, and number in the collection.[11] Such an alphabetical arrangement conforms to current practice in listing manuscripts and indeed is the only justifiable one. In item 2, for example, the two manuscripts are listed alphabetically, London before Oxford (for a few of the large libraries it is unnecessary, and a waste of space, to give the city every time). It is important, I believe, in

contrast to the practice of *IMEV* and other indexes, to give
both beginning *and* end folio numbers and manuscript dates
where available. Following the listing of the two manuscripts,
I give the main editions according to which manuscript or
manuscripts are used as the base, as in *IMEV*: thus the first
two are parallel editions of Titus and Bodley; the third is a
facsimile of Bodley only. It is unnecessary, I believe, to
give all printed editions in this section, as we would in
IMEP in Print: in this entry I have omitted Cockayne's and
Blake's editions.

The last section of the entry, which would be optional,
would contain additional information about the work that might
be useful to the reader. Item 5 is an example of what might
be included: for *IMEP in Print*, a list of other known manuscripts or, as in this case, another known version; cross-
references where relevant; perhaps some bibliography. Naturally, one would be selective about what to put into this section
and would use only information that is easily obtainable.

Now that I have discussed general principles of format
and have illustrated them by going through the straightforward
entries for *Hali Meidenhad*, I would like to turn to some
special problems that must be solved in the course of our work.
I will illustrate these problems primarily with examples from
my work on *IMEP in Print*, but the problems will be the same
in *IMEP*.

The first example involves multiple versions of a work--
in this case English translations of the Benedictine Rule
(items 4-6). It is clear that "None of the extant Middle
English versions is directly dependent on one of the others,
or translates literally a known Latin or French text,"[12] and
I have therefore listed them all separately. The information
at the end of item 5 seems to me to be important, and worth
including somewhere. I have added it only once, in item 5
because it is the oldest of the Middle English translations,
but have put the cross-reference "See also 5" in the other
entries. It would be too wasteful of space to put the information at the end of each entry. I have given Ker numbers for
the manuscripts of the Old English translations rather than
the manuscripts themselves both because it saves space and
because Ker is a standard *printed* work, but in *IMEP* perhaps
we should list the manuscripts themselves.

The Benedictine Rule is a fairly simple example of multiple versions, but there are more complicated ones. *Mandeville's Travels* is one that I have been working with recently.
There are four Middle English prose versions of the *Travels*,
which itself is a compilation originally written in French.
According to the latest studies,[13] these four versions are
not by a single translator but in fact have quite different

origins: (1) the so-called Defective Version (in thirty-four
manuscripts) is a "translation of a lost manuscript of the
Insular [French] Version, most closely related to subgroup
B (i)" (p. 194); (2) the Cotton version (one manuscript) is
a "conflation ... based on a lost manuscript of subgroup A
of the Defective Version ... by detailed reference to a manuscript of subgroup A of the Insular [French] Version" (p. 196);
(3) the Egerton version (one manuscript) is a "conflation ...
based on a lost manuscript of subgroup A of the Defective
Version and a lost English translation of [a Latin translation
of the Insular French Version subgroup A]" (pp. 196-97); and
(4) the Bodley version (two manuscripts) is "an abridgment
of the lost English translation of the [Latin translation
just mentioned]" (p. 197). These details are complicated,
and Mandeville scholars may be in disagreement about them,
but the existence of four distinct English versions is something that the indexer of Middle English prose must acknow-
ledge, and each version must therefore be listed separately,
with a cross-reference to the other prose translations as well
as to the two verse translations listed in the *Supplement* to
IMEV.

My second example is less complex than the first, but it
raises an important and even more complicated question. The
example involves, again, multiple versions, but this time by
the same author. Here *IMEV* provides the model: if two or
more versions of a work are by one author, then list them in
a single entry, with a separate subdivision for each, as in
the entries for Chaucer's *Legend of Good Women*, *Piers Plowman*,
and the *Confessio Amantis*. I would modify the model only by
giving as a separate entry the first line of the second version (and of the third if there is one) when it differs substantively from the first, with a cross-reference to the main
entry. The example I use is Richard Rolle's *Meditations on
the Passion* (item 9), which exists in two versions, both by
Rolle according to Hope Emily Allen.[14] Since I have not yet
seen all five manuscripts, I give only the entry that will
appear in *IMEP in Print*. The first line is from the earlier
version, the A-text; I have cross-referenced the first lines
of the relevant editions of the revised version, the B-text
(items 10-12). As an experiment, I have given the dates of
the base manuscripts in parentheses, just to see whether it
would be worth including such information in *IMEP in Print*
(I assume there is no question about doing so in *IMEP*). The
argument for including them in this case is that none of the
manuscripts of either version are contemporary with the
writing of the work; the argument against is that one need
not bother with manuscript dates in an *IMEP in Print*--not to
mention the time it would take to determine the latest opinion

on dates, which may be quite different from those given in
very old editions.

The entry itself is straightforward enough, but the question it raises is difficult: how best to deal with extracts
from a single work. I have looked at a good many examples
of extracts in *IMEV*, and I think the general principle there
is: if the extract appears as a separate poem (848.5, 1418.5,
1422.1, 1926.5, 2577.5), or is incorporated in another poem
(3535), or is signed by an author who is someone other than
the original author (745), then it is given a separate entry,
but with a cross-reference to the poem from which it is taken;
all other items are listed as supplementary items within the
main entry. This is a good principle (though unfortunately
not carried out consistently).[15] Moreover, and this is the
problem, in practice it is very difficult to decide just what
is a separate poem, as I know from having examined extracts
from the *Pricke of Conscience*. For example, *IMEV* has an "extract of twenty-eight lines ... occurring separately" as item
3561, but the extract from the Thornton manuscript, which
IMEV lists as a supplementary item within the main *Pricke of
Conscience* entry (3428), also occurs separately, beginning
at the very top of the first column of one page (f. 276va)
and ending two-thirds of the way down the first column of the
next (f. 277a), with the rest of the page blank. The same is
true of the other five extracts listed as supplementary items.
Can one really say that there is any difference in these
items that would justify one as a separate poem and the others
as extracts under the main *Pricke of Conscience* heading?[16]
I think not. There seem to me to be two possible ways to
deal realistically and usefully with extracts, whether they
are in prose or verse. The first is to list them in the main
entry, either along with the other manuscripts with a note
that they are extracts or as a separate category if there are
many of them, but with their first lines listed at the proper
alphabetical places elsewhere in the *Index* and with cross-
references to the main entry. The second is to index them
all as separate entries, with cross-references to the main
entry (and of course cross-references in the subject index
at the end of the book). I incline to the second of these
as a general principle because it seems to me more in keeping
with the way the Middle Ages viewed extracts, but there will
doubtless be cases where it would be better to group them
under the main entry (in *IMEV* the *Canterbury Tales* that appear
separately and the stories from the *Confessio Amantis* that
appear separately are two examples), and there may be practical
considerations in *IMEP*--space, for example--that would even
argue for the first as a general principle. But whichever
way we finally decide upon, the important result will be that

the first lines of all extracts will be listed in alphabetical
order, unlike *IMEV*, so that the reader interested in identifying an unknown piece will have as much information at his dis-
posal as possible.

As a final example, let me take a work that is well known,
the *Ancrene Riwle*, the indexing of which will show how much
must be brought to bear in deciding how best to prepare an
entry. The *Ancrene Riwle* is almost certainly a unique case,
but it is still a good example because it raises questions
that have to be answered with all works that exist in multiple
copies and, especially, in various revisions. From which
manuscript do we take the first line? How do we decide which
manuscripts should be listed in the main entry and which
should have separate entries? Which would take precedence:
similarity of first line or similarity of text?

First of all, the first line. One of the general principles of format is that the first line should come from the
earliest edition for *IMEP in Print*, which in this case would
be Morton's edition of the Nero manuscript for the Camden
Society, and from the first manuscript in alphabetical order
for the final *Index*, which in this case would be the Corpus
manuscript. In view of E.J. Dobson's recent work, however,
Cleopatra seems to be the oldest and closest survivor of the
author's original and may have been corrected by the author
himself, whom Dobson calls Scribe B,[17] while Corpus, which
is slightly later than Cleopatra, represents "the author's
own final and definitive revision of his work."[18] Since there
is no critical edition of the work (and may never be in view
of the difficulties involved in preparing one), one ought to
choose the first line from one of these two manuscripts. I
choose Cleopatra because, with Scribe B's corrections, I believe it brings us closer to the original than Corpus. For
item 13 I was tempted to omit Dobson's "[þe]" entirely to reflect his sense that Scribe B had erased it to bring the text
more in line with the original, but decided that that would
be taking too many liberties with the printed text.[19] When
we put together *IMEP*, however, we may want to make changes in
Dobson's transcription since the final state of the manuscript
page does not have þe; I have done this in the first line
for item 14.

For the entry itself I decided, first, that similarity of
text was more important than similarity of first line and,
second--and this is more controversial because it involves a
judgment on my part that would be impossible to prove--that
I would include all versions in which the scribe, or adapter,
or reviser was clearly conscious that he was taking an extant
work and making either small or large changes in it. The
texts and first lines of Nero and Cleopatra are similar, and

the same is true of Vernon in item 14. Titus begins imperfectly, but it too is closely related to the other three, as
is the fragment now at the Bodleian. These five therefore
present no problem: they all clearly belong together in the
main entry.

The situation is not so clear-cut with the other manuscripts. If Corpus is a revised version, should it not be
listed in a separate subdivision of the main entry, like the
revised and expanded version of Rolle's *Meditations* in item
9? At first I thought so, but decided otherwise for one important reason, dealt with at length by Dobson in his article
in the Tolkien *Festschrift*: that the manuscripts have so many
interconnections that the only way to account for them is to
assume that "The community remained in touch with the author,
and from him received additions to the basic text which were
inserted, not very systematically, into individual manuscripts,
but were liable to drop out and be either lost or put back in
the wrong places."[20] Dobson speculates that these additions
were either "composed and circulated in the obvious way, on
separate sheets of vellum," or added in the margins of individual manuscripts, as, for example, in Cleopatra, and were
then fixed by the author in Corpus, his final revision.[21]
Vernon, for example, which I have already placed in the main
entry, follows the expanded text in Corpus for some of Part
VIII, as does the Latin translation; another series of additions are common to Corpus, Vernon, the Latin translation,
and Pepys, the fourteenth-century Wycliffite revision; and
there are other examples of cross-collation.[22] With so many
interconnections among the manuscripts--not to mention that
the text in Corpus is closely related to the text in the
others and that the first line in Corpus is similar to that
in Nero, Cleopatra, and Vernon--I think it makes more sense
to put Corpus into the main entry with the other five.

Pepys is more difficult because it is an extensively rewritten version made in the fourteenth century by someone
other than the original author for a Lollard audience of men
and women and might therefore warrant a separate entry, but
the first line is similar to that in the other manuscripts
(it is not until some sixty-three words into the text that
one discovers that Pepys has omitted thirteen words--the
reference to "mine leove sustren"--that appear in the other
manuscripts already in the main entry), the text is related
to Titus (sometimes even showing the true reading where Titus
has the wrong one), and the adapter follows the eight-part
structure and the order of the text of the original, probably
because that is the easiest way to disguise his controversial
interpolations. Even the title, *Recluse*, did not persuade me
to index Pepys as a separate entry, for it is very close to

the one in Vernon, *Þe Roule of Reclous*, and, if we can judge
from the *Promptorium Parvulorum*, *recluse* was considered a
synonym of *anker*, the masculine form of the word used in the
title to the *Ancrene Riwle*. I therefore list Pepys in the
main entry.

Caius is the most difficult of all, for it has a different first line from the others and presents a "considerably
modified and rearranged" text[23]--Dobson calls it "extracts"[24]
--and my inclination, as I said earlier, would be to list all
extracts as separate items. But Caius follows closely the
actual wording of the text and "has high value, for the parts
which it includes, as a witness to the original text,"[25] and
for me these arguments tip the scales in favor of including
it in the main entry. As with all extracts, however, it
should have its first line entered as a separate entry (item
16) with a cross-reference to the main entry. Titus and the
Lanhydrock/Robartes fragment, on the other hand, are copies
of the basic text that begin imperfectly, and thus their
first lines should not be cross-referenced.

In contrast to these eight manuscripts, however, the last
remaining one, the Royal manuscript, which is a "free adaptation of the original [Parts II and III] to a lay audience"
made in the mid-fifteenth century perhaps by the famous
London preacher William Lichfield,[26] is clearly a "new" work:
a fifteenth-century hand calls it "optimus tractus de v sen-
sibus" in a list of contents on the beginning flyleaf, in the
text itself the work is referred to as a treatise in two parts,
and the opening "Omni custodia" comes back at the end, indi-
cating that the author thinks of the two parts as a unified
work, independent of its original. I have therefore entered
it separately, as item 17, but with a cross-reference to the
main *Ancrene Riwle* entry. I have done the same with the
Tretyse of Love (item 19), which is often included in lists
of *Ancrene Riwle* manuscripts: it is a compilation of ten
devotional tracts translated from French in the late fifteenth
century, the first three of which borrow from the *Ancrene
Riwle*; but the borrowings are random and are put into an entirely new context, quite different from the original.[27]

What I want to convey by the example of the *Ancrene Riwle*,
as well as the others, is that the indexing of Middle English
prose is more than just writing down first lines. It involves
judgments that go far beyond the mechanical and clerical aspects of the task and should be based on the most recent, most
authoritative scholarship. The difference between the *Ancrene
Riwle* and, say, *Mandeville's Travels* is partly in the nature
of the two works and partly in the nature of the scholarship
on the two works. The manuscripts of the *Ancrene Riwle* all
go back ultimately to a common original written in English by

an Englishman, very few manuscripts of the work exist, there
are many interconnections among them, and *Ancrene Riwle*
scholars have traditionally kept them together in a group.
Mandeville's Travels, on the other hand, appears in hundreds
of manuscripts in a number of languages, of which there are
at least six English versions in forty manuscripts, and
Mandeville scholars have spent a great deal of time and effort
distinguishing versions and trying to sort out their origins.
The nature of the two works and the nature of the scholarship
on the two works have determined for me that they should be
treated in the *Index* in different ways, even though at first
glance they may seem to present identical problems. Making
the necessary distinctions between such works and preparing
the entries based on these distinctions is a time-consuming
process, but perhaps that is as it should be in an *Index* that
aspires to serve the whole scholarly community of medievalists
in the fullest, most informative way possible.[28]

Robert E. Lewis
Indiana University

NOTES

1. Indexing by manuscript collection is, of course,
another possible way, and in fact will be used as the organizational device for Stage 2 of the project--the Handlists of
individual collections--but it is an arbitrary device, really
having nothing to do with the prose itself; moreover, since
the *Index* should include pre-1500 works that exist only in
print (like the *Tretyse of Love* and one of the English translations of the Benedictine Rule that I will have occasion to
mention later on), manuscript collection is not an all-inclusive category.

2. From this point on, when I use "*Index*" or "Indexes" I
mean both *IMEP in Print* and *IMEP*.

3. The first volume of its predecessor, Carleton Brown's
Register (Oxford, 1916), which has still not been superseded,
was devoted entirely to a list of manuscripts containing
English verse, and most scholarly books published nowadays
have a list of manuscripts cited, e.g., those by Jolliffe
and Revell.

4. Thus I have retained the ampersand in item 4, but I
have expanded the barred-7 sign in items 1 and 2 as *et* and
the same sign in item 5 as *and*.

5. In Preston's *Concordance* everything is strictly alphabetical, so that, for example, the Middle English equivalents
of Modern English *Lady/Ladies* appear under at least twenty-
six headings in various places in the L-section (La-, Le-,
Ll-, Lo-). *IMEV*, on the other hand, groups together (1832-1840)
all nine lines beginning with the Middle English equivalent
of Modern English *Lady* at the place where *Lady* comes alphabetically and then arranges the nine lines according to the
spelling of the second word; in addition, a cross-reference
appears at another common Middle English spelling, *Leuedi*.
This arrangement is more useful than to alphabetize within
the grouping according to the actual Middle English spelling
of the initial word. As an added convenience, however, it
might be possible to give the Modern English initial word in
the margin, as one finds in most concordances.

6. Jolliffe, for example, repeats lines that have changes
farther down the line (see the four lines for I.22(c) on
p. 178, especially the last two, or the seven lines for
H.16(c) on p. 180, especially the last five), but they seem
to me to serve no useful purpose (and in addition waste space),
for the manuscripts in each case are all grouped together in
the body of the checklist and thus apparently contain the
same text.

7. On the other hand, if it were a question of a different, perhaps revised, version of a work, as determined by the
most recent and authoritative scholarship, then I would give
both first lines even if the differences were not substantive.
The Prologue to Chaucer's *Legend of Good Women* is a revealing
example, and shows the difficulty of deciding what first lines
to index. The Prologue exists in two versions, an earlier
one (F) and a revised one (G), but the only difference in the
first lines is that F has *tymes* as its third word whereas G
has *sythes*. Since the two words are synonymous, one would
not normally index both lines, and in fact *IMEV* does not give
the line from G, simply noting that there is a second version
under the main heading (100). But the existence of a clearly
revised version of this Prologue seems to me to call for a
cross-reference of its first line, even though it is very
similar and even though it would appear only two entries
earlier in *IMEV* (between items 98 and 99).

8. E.J. Dobson, "The Date and Composition of *Ancrene Wisse*,"
Proceedings of the British Academy, 52 (1966), 192, 206, and
The Origins of Ancrene Wisse (Oxford, 1976), pp. 121 n. 2, 239.

9. For second editions, as in item 13, editions 3 and 7,
I have given the date in parentheses after the date of the
first; an exception is Furnivall's re-edition of *Hali Meidenhad*

for the Early English Text Society (hereafter EETS) (item 1,
edition 2), which is by a different editor and prints a new
manuscript in parallel columns beside the base manuscript of
the earlier edition. In no case have I given reprint dates,
which are interesting information but not really essential to
IMEP in Print; moreover, so many editions in the EETS have
been reprinted that it would be too cumbersome to list reprint
dates each time I list the original editions.

The only exception in the examples in the Appendix to
"editions of the complete work" is Shepherd's edition of
Parts VI and VII of the *Ancrene Riwle* (item 13, edition 7);
I have listed it primarily because the *Ancrene Riwle* has
never had a critical edition and because Shepherd's introduction and notes are so full. We have not yet decided what to
do in *IMEP in Print* about such partial editions or about selections of Middle English prose in the standard anthologies;
perhaps the anthologies could be listed, with numbers, at
the end of the Introduction and those numbers noted, where
appropriate, in the final, optional section of an entry.

10. Though I have given book titles in full in the examples
in the Appendix, in both printed Indexes there will of course
be abbreviations for such frequently cited items as *Yorkshire
Writers* and H.E. Allen's *English Writings of Richard Rolle*.

11. For each manuscript I have given the current location
and name, which I believe is the only justifiable way, even
if, at an earlier date or at the time of the edition, the
manuscript may have had a different location and name, though
I have tried to suggest something about earlier location and
ownership with the Lanhydrock/Robartes fragment of the *Ancrene
Riwle* now in the Bodleian Library (item 14, manuscript 8).

12. Charlotte D'Evelyn, "Instructions for Religious," in
A Manual of the Writings in Middle English, ed. J. Burke
Severs, 2 (New Haven, 1970), 461.

13. So far as I know, Appendix B to M.C. Seymour's edition
of *The Metrical Version of Mandeville's Travels*, EETS, o.s.
269 (London, 1973), is the most recent discussion of these
versions and the insular tradition in general--a discussion
based both on his own previous work and on that of others.
The information and quotations in this paragraph come from
Seymour's Appendix B.

14. *Writings Ascribed to Richard Rolle* (New York, 1927),
pp. 280-85, and *English Writings of Richard Rolle* (Oxford,
1931), pp. 17-18. But see Margery M. Morgan, "Versions of
the Meditations of the Passion Ascribed to Richard Rolle,"
Medium AEvum, 22 (1953), 100-101, 103, who says that Rolle's

authorship of both versions must remain an open question.   I
am indebted to Sister Mary Madigan of Loretto College, Toronto,
for the information in items 9.B.4 and 10 in the Appendix.

15. For the principle, and the examples, regarding extracts as separate poems, see the note at the end of the entry
for Chaucer's *Troilus and Criseyde* (3327) in the *Supplement*
to *IMEV*. The principle was apparently not articulated so
clearly in *IMEV*, for *Supplement* 1422.5 (five stanzas beginning
at I.400) was originally 3327 Extract D; moreover, it is not
clear how this item differs from 3327 Extracts B and J (one
stanza beginning at I.400). As for extracts incorporated in
another poem, the model is 3535 (also from *Troilus and
Criseyde*), where one finds the one known manuscript listed,
with a cross-reference at 3327; the inconsistency in this
case appears in the *Supplement*, where, although a second manuscript of 3535 has been discovered, it is not listed in the
item itself but only as 3327 Extract G.

16. Strangely, one of the six extracts (3428 Extract C)
has its first line cross-referenced in *IMEV* between items 492
and 493, though not the other five; in the *Supplement* the
first line of the Thornton extract (3428 Extract F) has been
added as a cross-reference between items 3306.8 and 3307.5,
though none of the others. Three additional extracts from the
Pricke of Conscience appear in *IMEV* (806, 2753, 3866), but
they are not identified as being from the *Pricke of Conscience*
and are listed as separate poems, for which see Derek Britton,
"Manuscripts Associated with Kirby Bellars Priory," *Transac-
tions of the Cambridge Bibliographical Society*, 6 (1976),
279-80, items 11, 12, and 19.

17. See "The Date and Composition of *Ancrene Wisse*," esp.
pp. 199-205, the Introduction (pp. ix, xciii-xcix, et passim)
to his edition of the Cleopatra manuscript (EETS, o.s. 267
[London,, 1972]), and· *The Origins of Ancrene Wisse*, pp. 238-
41, 259-64, 277-78, 285, and 317-18. See also John Bradford
Senden, "Manuscript, Audience and Text: A Study of the Relationships Between the Surviving Texts of the *Ancrene Riwle*"
(Indiana Univ. dissertation, 1978), pp. 27-43.

18. Dobson, "The Affiliations of the Manuscripts of
Ancrene Wisse," in *English and Medieval Studies Presented to
J.R.R. Tolkien*, ed. Norman Davis and C.L. Wrenn (London,
1962), p. 163.

19. See Dobson's discussion in n. 3 on p. 1 of his edition.

20. "Affiliations," p. 162.

21. Ibid., pp. 157 and 157-62 passim.

22. Ibid., pp. 137-57 passim.

23. R.M. Wilson, ed., *The English Text of the Ancrene Riwle*, EETS, o.s. 229 (London, 1954), p. xiv.

24. "Affiliations," p. 132.

25. Ibid. Caius has a title, *Contra Iram*, at the end of the first line of text on p. 1, but I have not added it to the list of titles in items 13 and 14 because I do not believe it is intended as a title to the whole work; it refers only to the discussion of anger from the beginning of Part III, which is where the extracts begin.

26. A.C. Baugh, ed., *The English Text of the Ancrene Riwle*, EETS, o.s. 232 (London, 1956), p. ix; see also the discussion on pp. ix-xi.

27. For *IMEP* there are two possible ways to treat this item: (1) to say "No MS extant," in in *IMEV*, and then to list both editions on the following line; or (2) to use Wynkyn de Worde's edition as the main witness and then to put J.H. Fisher's edition for EETS on the following line. Because *IMEP* is both a manuscript and an incunabulum index, I incline to the latter, but for reasons of internal consistency (as well as similarity to *IMEV*) perhaps the former is preferable. The same problem will occur with item 6 in the Appendix.

28. This paper is a revised version of the one I presented at the Cambridge Conference. Let me emphasize that it is a working paper only and that the editorial technique that I have described in it will be subject to constant modification as work on the *Index* progresses. I hope that readers will scrutinize the editorial technique carefully, especially as it is illustrated in the examples in the Appendix, and will send me suggestions about how it might be modified for the better, for all of us interested in Middle English studies have a stake in making the *Index* as useful and as full and as informative and as clear a tool as we can.

APPENDIX OF EXAMPLES CITED IN THE TEXT

1. AVDI filia et uide et inclina aurem tuam ... Dauið þe
    psalm wruhte spekeð i þe sawter towart godes spuse þet is
    euch meiden þet haueð meiið þeawes (from Bodley 34 in 2)

    [*Hali Meidenhad, Hali Meiðhad*] (*Epistel of Meidenhad*
    in Bodley 34 in 2 and 4), homiletic treatise, *ca.* 1200.

    1. EETS, o.s. 18 (1866) (B.L. Cotton Titus D.xviii, ff.
    112v-27); 2. EETS, o.s. 18, 2nd ed. (1922) (MS in 1 and
    Bodl. Bodley 34, ff. 52-71v, parallel); 3. *Hali Meiðhad*,
    ed. A.F. Colburn (1940) (as in 2, parallel); 4. EETS,
    o.s. 247 (1960), ff. 52-71v (facsimile of Bodley 34);
    5. ed. N.F. Blake, *Middle English Religious Prose* (1972),
    pp. 35-60 (MS in 4).

2. Avdi filia et uide et inclina aurem tuam ... Dauið þe
    psalm wruhte spekeð i þe sawter towart godes spuse þet
    is euch meiden þet haueð meiið þeawes (from 2)

    Epistel of Meidenhad (from 2) [*Hali Meidenhad, Hali
    Meiðhad*], homiletic treatise, *ca.* 1200.

    1. B.L. Cotton Titus D.xviii, ff. 112v-27, s. xiii[1]
    (2nd 1/4); 2. Bodl. Bodley 34, ff. 52-71v, s. xiii in.

    1,2. EETS, o.s. 18, 2nd ed. (1922); *Hali Meiðhad*, ed.
    A.F. Colburn (1940); 2. EETS, o.s. 247 (1960), ff. 52-
    71v (facsimile).

3. Dauið þe psalm wruhte spekeð þe sawter   See 1 (2 in
    IMEP).

4. Asculta o fili Son Herkyn þe commandementis of þe mastir
    & lay to þe eere of thy herte

    Reule of Sain Benet (trans. of Benedictine Rule), rule
    for religious (monks in prol. and chaps. 1-2, nuns
    thereafter), s. xv in. See also 5.

    EETS, o.s. 120 (1902), pp. 1-47 (B.L. Landsdowne 378,
    ff. 1v-42v).

5. Ausculta o filia precepta magistri ... ȝehur ðu min bearn
    beboda þines lareowes and onhyld þinre hurte eare and
    þines arfaestam faeder mynaȝunga lustlice underfoh

    Reȝolan Sanctes Benedictes (trans. of Benedictine Rule),
    rule made for nuns of Winteney, with Latin and English
    interspersed, 1200-1225.

Ed. M.M.A. Schröer, *Die Winteney-Version der Regula S. Benedicti* (1888) (B.L. Cotton Claudius D.iii, ff. 50-138)

Another version (for women) in Washington, Library of Congress 4, ff. 1-36, s. xv; for other versions in print see *IMEV* 218 and *IMEP in Print* 4 and 6. Another translation made for the nuns of Winteney in 1516 by Bishop Richard Fox (R. Pynson [1516?], STC 1859). For OE translations, see (1) Ker 41B, 109, 117, 154B, 186 item 25, 200, 353; (2) Ker 395; (3) Ker 186 item 1.

6. He or she þat is to be made hede or souereyn in a monestary in whom alle the hole congregacion in one acorde after god consentyth

   Rule of Saynte Benet (an abstract, trans. of Benedictine Rule), rule for men and women, s. xv ex. See also 5.

   1. William Caxton [1491] (STC 3305), with prefatory material; 2. EETS, o.s. 120 (1902), pp. 119-40 (as in 1).

7. 3ehur ðu min bearn beboda þines lareowes   See 5.

8. Son Herkyn þe commandementis of þe mastir   See 4.

9. Swete lord Jesu Cryst I thanke þe and 3elde þe graces of þat swete prayere and of þat holy orysoun þat þou madest

   Richard Rolle, [*Meditations on the Passion*] (*Meditacio de Passione Domini* in A, *Devoute Meditaciouns of þe Passioun of Christ* in B1, *A Devout Meditacion up þe Passioun of Crist* in B3, *Meditacio Passionis Iesu Christi* in B4), s. xiv[1].

   A text (the original): 1. *ES*, 7 (1884), 454-63, with corrections in *ES*, 12 (1889), 463-68 (C.U.L. Ll.1.8, ff. 201-207v, s. xiv ex.); 2. *Yorkshire Writers*, I (1895), 83-91 (as in 1); 3. ed. H.E. Allen, *English Writings of Richard Rolle* (1931), pp. 19-27 (as in 1).

   B text (longer, revised version): 1. *Yorkshire Writers*, I (1895), 92-103 (C.U.L. Add. 3042, ff. 36-78v, s. xv); 2. ed Harald Lindkvist, *Skrifter utgifna af K. Humanistika Vetenskaps-Samfundet i Uppsala*, 19,3 (1917) (Uppsala Univ. C 494, ff. 1-32, s. xv in.), beginning imperfectly; 3. ed H.E. Allen, *English Writings of Richard Rolle* (1931), pp. 27-36 (Bodl. e Mus. 232, ff. 1v-8, s. xv); 4. ed. Mary F. Madigan, *The Passio Domini Theme in the Works of Richard Rolle* (1978), pp. 236-77 (B.L. Cotton Titus C.xix, ff. 92v-117v, s. xv ex.).

Cross-reference to *A Talkyng of the Love of God*, which is an imitation of the *Meditations*.

10. Lord as thou made me of noȝt J be seche the ȝeue me grace to serue the with alle my herte   See 9.B.4.

11. LOrd þat made [me] and hast yeven me many yiftis gostly bodily and worldly I beseche þe graunt me grace to use ham al   See 9.B.3.

12. LOrd þat madist me of nouȝt I biseche þee to ȝeue me grace to serue þe wiþ al myn herte   See 9.B.1.

13. Recti diligunt te ... Lauerd seið godes spuse to hire deore wurðe spus þeo richte luuieð þe þeo beoð [þe] richte þe liuieð efter riwle (from 11)

    [*Ancrene Riwle*] (*Ancrene Wisse* in 4, 7, and 8; *Recluse* in 3 and 12), guide for nuns, s. xiii in. (probably 1215-1222).

    1. Camden Soc. 57 (1853) (B.L. Cotton Nero A.xiv, ff. 1-120v); 2. *Journal of Germanic Philology*, 2 (1898), 199-202 (Bodl. Eng. th. c. 70, ff. 1-1v), fragment; 3. *The Recluse*, ed. J. Påhlsson, *Lunds Univ. Årsskrift*, N.F., Afd. 1, Bd. 6, Nr. 1 (1911, 2nd ed. 1918) (Camb. Magdalene Pepys 2498, pp. 371a-449a), 14th-c. Wycliffite revision; 4. *Ancrene Wisse*, ed. A.R. Jewett (Cornell Univ. diss., 1936) (Camb. Corpus Christi 402, ff. 1-117v), revised version; 5. EETS, o.s. 225 (1952) (as in 1); 6. EETS, o.s. 229 (1954) (Camb. Gonville and Caius 234/120, pp. 1-185), extracts, rearranged; 7. *Ancrene Wisse*, Parts VI and VII, ed. G. Shepherd (1959, 2nd ed. 1972) (as in 4); 8. EETS, o.s. 249 (1962) (as in 4); 9. EETS, o.s. 252 (1963), pp. 1-160 (B.L. Cotton Titus D.xviii, ff. 14a-105b), beginning imperfectly at end of Part I; 10. EETS, o.s. 252 (1963), pp. 166-67 (as in 2); 11. EETS, o.s. 267 (1972) (B.L. Cotton Cleopatra C.vi, ff. 4-198v); 12. EETS, o.s. 274 (1976) (as in 3).

    Also in Bodl. Eng. poet. a. 1 (Vernon MS), ff. 339vb-93b. French translations in B.L. Cotton Vitellius F.vii (EETS, o.s. 219 [1944]) and Camb. Trinity R.14.7, Bodl. Bodley 90, and Paris B.N. français 6276 (EETS, o.s. 240 [1958]; Latin trans. in B.L. Cotton Vitellius E.vii, B.L. Royal 7 C.x, Oxf. Magdalen 67, and Oxf. Merton 44 (EETS, o.s. 216 [1944]).

14. Recti diligunt te ... Lauerd seið godes spuse to hire
     deore wurðe spus þeo richte Luuieð þe þeo beoð richte
     þe liuieð efter riwle (from 4)

> [*Ancrene Riwle*] (*Ancrene Wisse* in 1, *Recluse* in 3, *Þe
> Roule of Reclous* in 7), guide for nuns, s. xiii in.
> (probably 1215-1222).

> 1. Camb. Corpus Christi 402, ff. 1-117v, *ca.* 1230 (re-
> vised version); 2. Camb. Gonville and Caius 234/120,
> pp. 1-185, s. xiii^2 (extracts, rearranged); 3. Camb.
> Magdalene Pepys 2498, pp. 371a-449a, s. xiv^2 (Wycliffite
> revision); 4. B.L. Cotton Cleopatra C.vi, ff. 4-198v,
> 1225-30; 5. B.L. Cotton Nero A.xiv, ff. 1-120v, s.
> xiii^1 (prob. 2nd 1/4); 6. B.L. Cotton Titus D.xviii,
> ff. 14a-105b, s. xiii^1 (2nd 1/4); 7. Bodl. Eng. poet.
> a. 1 (Vernon MS), ff. 339vb-93b), s. xiv ex. (after
> 1382); 8. Bodl. Eng. th. c. 70, ff. 1-1v, s. xiv^1 (Lan-
> hydrock/Robartes fragment).

> Then would follow a list of editions, by number as in
> the *Hali Meidenhad* entry (retaining 13.1 but omitting
> 13.2-4, 7), and probably a list of the French and
> Latin MSS, as in 13 above.

15. Lauerd seið godes spuse to hire deore wurðe spus   See
     13 (14 in *IMEP*).

16. O her ageynes wartþe monie remedies frowern a muchel
     floch and mistliche boten   See 13.6 (14.2 in *IMEP*).

17. Omni custodia serua cor tuum ... With alle warde kep þin
     hert for of hit lyfe goþe þese are þe wordys of Salomon

> William Lichfield (?), *Tractus de V Sensibus* (based on
> Parts II and III of the *Ancrene Riwle*), s. xv med.
> See 13.

> EETS, o.s. 232 (1956) (B.L. Royal 8 C.i, ff. 122v-43v).

18. With alle warde kep þin hert   See 17.

19. This tretyse is of loue and spekyth of iiij of the most
     specyall louys that ben in the worlde

> *Tretyse of Love*, compilation of devotional tracts
> translated from French (based in part on the *Ancrene
> Riwle*), 1493. See 13.

> 1. Wynkyn de Worde, 1493 (STC 24234); 2. EETS, o.s.
> 223 (1951) (as in 1).

PROBLEMS IN RECORDING THE CONTENTS
OF THE COSIN MANUSCRIPTS

The Cosin collection includes eighty-one of the eighty-nine medieval manuscript codices in Durham University Library and is named after John Cosin, Bishop of Durham from 1660 to 1672, founder of the Episcopal Library now administered by the University.[1] He himself collected only a handful of them, the bulk in fact being given by one of his chaplains, George Davenport, Rector of Houghton-le-Spring, who died in 1677, having acquired them between 1652 and 1670 in various parts of England, and all but a couple originated there.[2] Twenty-five contain some Middle English, twenty-one of them prose. One is a New Testament, one a Lollard dialogue, one consists of two translations of pseudo-Bonaventure, one is a copy of Mirk's *Festial*, one is an autograph of Thomas Hoccleve, two have legends of saints, one is a schoolmaster's book, another a parish priest's, and so on, affording a fairly wide variety, although not the full range of possibilities. Seven include medical and culinary recipes; I have not attempted as yet a complete inventory of their contents, in view of Dr. Hargreaves' paper on the former category (see below pp. 91-113) and work in progress by two other specialists on the latter material.[3] I have the advantage of knowing the manuscripts I chose for the experiment, ten in all, and their contents (predominantly religious) quite well, since I have been looking after them now for nearly twenty-eight years, have outlined general descriptions of them, and can bring to bear on them my personal kinds of interest.

At the discussion of the present project which I attended in York in 1977, when it was suggested that I address the problems of listing the Middle English prose contents of a particular collection, I promised to produce a trial pro-forma which could be employed by other collaborators. Having failed hitherto, I have now devised something of the sort through applying some of the procedures outlined in the cyclostyled "Guide for the Preparation of Index Entries" which Professor Edwards circulated in advance of this meeting. (I will refer to this from now on as the "Guide.") A study of the "Guide" raised other questions, especially concerning how much we can

afford to make of the Handlist stage of the project. I am
convinced that the proposal to list collection by collection,
manuscript by manuscript, item after item, leaf by leaf, word
after word, does most fortunately postpone many difficult
decisions about arranging, abbreviating, and standardizing
the information recorded, until at least the completion of
each collection or of a larger group of these Handlists. It
also allows beneficial latitude for individual contributors
to exercise their discretion and to learn from their own and
others' experience as to the amounts of comparative investigation and of incidental detail which may be useful and manageable.
Certainly, as many editors and compilers must realize too late,
it is best at the stage of initial record to include more
rather than less of what is in front of you, provided that the
main purpose is not unduly obscured or delayed. The organizers
have already circulated a request for additional information
concerning the decoration of manuscripts. It was of course
envisaged as a gratuitous by-product, but we should ask ourselves at the beginning whether there are simple observations,
relevant to the future utility of the Handlists and possible
indexes,[4] which we would do well to incorporate and our omitting of which might be a cause of regret later. It is obvious
that these Handlists cannot give complete descriptions of the
manuscripts involved, even of those portions of them containing
Middle English prose, but there are some facts and opinions
which could assist students of this very material from one
point of view and which we ought therefore to offer, in a manner which indicates the character of the evidence or authority
and allows for the varying competence and confidence of the
contributors.

     It is in order to help contributors to be sufficiently full
yet no longer than requisite, and to make their work both faster
and more consistent, that some sort of pro-forma is desirable,
not as a straight-jacket but as an *aide-mémoire*, together with
guidance in conventions of transcribing and summarizing, if
the eventual indexers and interim users are not to have excessive
doubts and difficulties. The form (appended) I have devised
for discussion, based on the listing of Cosin manuscripts and a
good deal of listing and indexing of others for similar purposes
previously, provides three sheets of A4 paper (if necessary
both sides) for each prose item to be listed, and I think it
would be a mistake to try to do with less, for an unpredictable
number of items will require most of the space in one or more
of the sections and a few may over-run it. Some of the points
I have put down may be unexpected but they are there primarily
for textual, not palaeographical, value.

     I scarcely suppose anyone will wish to dispute the first
four lines on sheet A, for the names of the locality, library,

collection and the call number, and catalogue references.[5]
The item number (as requested in the preliminary "Guide"), if
it were that within the whole sequence of a miscellany in more
than one language or genre, especially when still uncatalogued
or inadequately or contradictorily itemized in an existing
catalogue (as is not at all uncommon), could cause a lot of
work and trouble. I take it that the numeration should be by
the items in each manuscript qualifying for our record (i.e.,
including some which, containing only small quantities of
English prose, may not be finally *indexed*[6]), which would also
permit differing from ones adopted by previous cataloguers,
determined by our own observations, knowledge, or convenience.
For instance, in Cosin V.IV.4, a legend of St. Barbara in sixteen chapters is followed by a collection of her miracles,
which, from their respective explicit and incipit rubrics,
might not be so coupled elsewhere, though in fact they are so
in the only other copies at present known, incorporated in the
Lambeth 72 *Gilte Legende*.[7] In any case it would be more pru-
dent to number the life and the miracles distinctly, for the
sake of separate indexing of their incipits; and as there is
no prologue or express shape or extent to the collection of
miracles it is also necessary to decide if the beginning and
ending of each miracle must be quoted (with a subsidiary item
number or letter), or whether a summary, for an eventual motif
index, may suffice.[8]

The majority of the space on sheet A is provided for the
beginning and ending of the item, continued over if necessary.
I think it best to say on what precise page the item begins
before quoting, for its incipit may run beyond a recto or verso
on to the next, and if so, it may be wise also to mark where
that occurs. I assume we are agreed that it is economical and
safer to dispense with little *r* for recto if one employs little
v for verso. In the "Guide" it was suggested that we transcribe all manuscript quotations verbatim, but to ignore manuscript punctuation and capitalization. I fear that is too
curt, and we must decide whether we want a slightly edited or
a more or less diplomatic transcript and, whichever it is to
be, specify the conventions in greater detail. In my test run
I found it too distracting to have to decide what I was to
suppress, supply, or alter as I went along, and I believe it
will be simpler, at least when copying directly from the manuscript (alternatively from a microfilm), to conform as closely
as possible to what is there, the exact function or interpretation of which is not yet settled, even if it has to be edi-
torially modified in the later typescript. It is not always
easy to identify and represent medieval punctuation and capitalization, but it is not very satisfactory to remove them
without substituting alternatives, and it might nowadays or in

the future be thought by some to be retrograde not to give
such clues to those interested in this aspect of Middle
English prose (not merely palaeographers) when we could do so
by recording relatively few simply reproducible signs.[9] We
need also to know if abbreviations are to be expanded silently
or not, according to some authoritative system, if we are to
reduce divergences as far as possible.[10] Inconsistencies in
spelling are of course inevitable between one item, manuscript,
or list and another, following the more or less regular behavior
of the scribes and our collaborators. These differences mostly
may not matter when they come to be alphabetically indexed if
modern spelling is taken as the norm for that purpose, whenever
possible, as I have supposed will be done on the precedent of
the *Index of Middle English Verse*. But the usefulness of the
Handlists for a variety of legitimate entries (to which the
indexing is, after all, only itself an aid) will be affected
by the degree to which the enquirers are able to rely on the
details of the reports: not, of course, as a substitute for
looking at the manuscripts, but to see which manuscripts, and
what parts of them, may first merit looking at in pursuit of
a particular interest. The reporter will have to assess the
usages of the scribes of his beginnings and endings in other
parts of each item or manuscript to know how specific abbreviations may be expanded, or if they are otiose strokes. In response to arguments by Professor McIntosh and Dr. Benskin about
the graphemic significance, as well as to save ourselves some
time and hesitation, it might be prescribed that such forms as
"wᵗ" and "þᵗ" should be preserved, and that *y* employed for *þ*
should *not* be converted to the latter.[11] The more unusual
idiosyncrasies of spelling, as well as probable errors, will
demand the use of [sic]. Where dittography, for instance, is
suspected it seems to me that the Handlists had better say
[sic], where an edition of the text would correct it, and our
final indexers will also be in a better position to do so.

Furthermore, how are we to indicate cancellations and
alterations which affect word order and sense, which may be
close in date or of comparable authority with the original?
There are well-established conventions for showing such changes,
and we must adopt some or provide our own.[12] In Cosin V.III.24,
which contains t.ree treatises concerning contemplative life,
a contemporary corrector who was equipped to supply quite long,
apparently authentic passages skipped by the original scribes
also makes smaller verbal alterations which therefore have a
strong claim to be quoted.[13] Contrariwise, in Cosin V.IV.6,
with two other devotional treatises, a hand somewhat later
than the original makes changes, including erasures, which
look much more arbitrary. No doubt we will normally, in the
course of our quotations, disregard post-medieval tinkerings

with the text, such as censorship of popery and modernization
of vocabulary, although we *may* want to note their presence,
date, and authorship, but if they declare or show symptoms of
derivation from another medieval copy, we ought to record some
of them verbatim, just as, when we have alternative readings
in medieval hands, we must choose to quote one or both and ex-
plain clearly what we are doing, particularly if our practice
differs from item to item or Handlist to Handlist. An existing
edition of a text or study of the manuscript may help us to
assess the significance of such alterations, but we are left
with the problems of presentation.

To transcribe at least fifty words at the beginning of each
item may seem to be more than will be requisite for identification and indexing in most cases, but it is not possible to be
sure without them, as it depends greatly on the structure of
each beginning, which may vary from copy to copy of the same
text. Several quotations of up to fifty words may indeed be
needed to cope with prefatory prayers, prologues, and contents
lists which can occur in different orders before the opening of
the main text, or undergo modifications. As an example, in
Cosin V.III.5, Mirk's *Festial*, there is a prayer before the prologue, followed by the opening of the first sermon; this is hard
to accommodate at all adequately in one total of fifty words.[14]
Another example, Cosin V.V.12, item 2, has a short title, "The
meditacion of Jordan of the lyfe and passion of iesu criste,"
followed by an invocation including a longer description and
attribution, then a lengthy prologue of seven pages before the
first article of a series of sixty-five. As Professor Edwards
has said and exemplified, "On occasion it is not possible to
distinguish with certainty between a preliminary rubric and
the actual beginning of a work."[15] Moreover, the exact wording
of the rubrics, with the numbering and order of chapters (for
instance, Walter Hilton's translation of the *Stimulus Amoris*
in Cosin V.III.8 or the *Contemplations of the Dread and Love
of God* in Cosin V.IV.6), can be among the distinguishing
features of variant recensions, besides providing contemporary
titles and ascriptions of authorship (as in Cosin V.III.8).[16]
The decision now to "include all opening rubrics or seeming
rubrics" makes the task of the contributor straightfoward
though lengthier. Which of these various incipits may merit
eventual alphabetical indexing is a comparative and utilitarian
judgment, tackled all the better at later stages.

It is also not easy to know which pious invocations,
sayings, or verses, Latin, English, or French, preceding or
following an item, are likely to be found with more than the
copy in hand, unless there is already a published edition or
study, and it may not be clear from that. "Iesus Maria" at
the head of an epistle in Cosin V.III.16 might well be omitted,

whether one decides that the item qualifies for indexing as a
piece of spiritual counsel or solely for record as an actual
missive with the volume,[17] though in either case such invocation
is a customary accompaniment of a letter for some writers, as
it is for a book by some copyists. Likewise, "Iesus est amor
meus" at the end of an extract from the *Mirror of St. Edmund*,
item 2 in Cosin V.IV.6; whereas "Ardeat in nobis divini fervor
amoris" at the beginning and end of item 1, the *Contemplations
of the Dread and Love of God*, occurs with enough other copies
and is sufficiently distinctive to be regarded as integral,
though if the reporter did not have this information, he might
be in doubt. If in doubt, include it, is the safest advice.
The General Editors can easily excise it later, or an indexer
ignore it.

There are, incidentally, some optional observations I
myself would like to see, on sheet B or C, about the presence
or absence of rubrics describing the contents, particularly
of the chapters, of any item--and I should say that I am using
the word "rubric" in this paper as has been done in the "Guide,"
without regard to the actual color of ink employed for such
headings, etc. Not infrequently some or all are omitted, even
though space has been provided for them by the copyists, and
this is a defect which deserves note in proportion to its extent, as I assume other substantial defects will receive.
Sometimes, however, the spaces provided are insufficient for
the rubrics, which overflow more than a little into the margins.
When this has happened, it may be that the scribe of the
rubric (who may or may not be the same as for the main text
and, if not, may be much later) was either employing a different
exemplar or else improvising because he did not have one for
those words. The significance is like that of alterations,
derived or invented.

To return to sheet A, it was suggested in the "Guide" and
specimens that the transcription of the ending of an item (to
start before any formulaic phrases) should be given immediately
after that of the beginning. (The page number of an ending
should of course be that of the very last word quoted and best
follows it, to avoid any doubt.) There is, however, something
to be said for putting between the two quotations, rather than
on sheet B, where I have allowed for them, some statements
about the content and structure of an item which has not been
identified with an edited or well-studied work. Wherever we
put them, I suggest specifying for unidentified items, and especially for those defective at the beginning, not only the
number of chapter or rubric divisions, or *distinctiones* (numbered points) in shorter pieces, but also the first and last
scriptural, patristic, or other *auctoritas, sententia*, or
exemplum, as clues to be checked elsewhere.[18] If the last

item in Cosin V.V.12 had not had its prefatory title, invocation, and final rubric, its source could have been identified, despite the multitude of different meditations on the Passion of Christ, by the number of its articles, and if it were more defective at the end than it is, by their structure and subdivision.[19] Item 2 in V.IV.6, headed only "Contemplacio in deo," can be identified from its opening distinction and citation of St. Augustine, and the pattern of meditation on the Manhood and Godhood proposed to be an extract of St. Edmund Rich's *Mirror of the Church*--but to say whether it corresponds with any of the various complete and partial translations of that work, mostly still unpublished, will necessitate close comparisons with more than the fifty opening and closing words and is therefore beyond what can be expected of a Handlist, although a well-placed contributor may sometimes be able to do more.[20]

On sheets B and C, the repetition of the basic manuscript details at the top is a precaution against the dossier on one item being dispersed. The title of the item on sheet B may also be simply repeated from one conspicuous in the transcription on sheet A or it may come from somewhere else in the text or a running head, either original or added. These should be given as quotations (with indication of source) if they differ substantially from each other or from alternatives in other manuscripts, editions, or studies, which are not necessarily more authoritative (since they are sometimes modern inventions) and may not need to be spelled out fully here if they are in the bibliographical citations below or on the back of the same sheet. Ascriptions of authorship in the manuscript, if original or medieval, should always be quoted or summarized at this point, with any correction from other sources. Post-medieval titles and attributions found in the manuscript may also be quoted, with approximate dates, if they seem to be very early or well informed; they will be found in volume contents lists as well as on the item in question--I think of many in the Cosin manuscripts by George Davenport's hand, like those by his colleague and correspondent William Sancroft in Emmanuel, Lambeth, and Tanner manuscripts--because they *might* be taken from another (perhaps now lost) medieval source, but more often than not probably from the unreliable Bale or Pits. As an example of both points, item 1 of Cosin V.IV.6, the *Contemplations of the Dread and Love of God* as it is styled in the printed editions (not in the manuscripts), has no obvious original title, but one is added in the top margin of its first page by the late fifteenth-century tinkerer with its text, "þe goldyn ross," and, after an interval (in the same hand but different ink) "drawen owtt of þe trew love," both of which I think qualify for quotation, while a mid-sixteenth-century hand has appended

"Of the love of god," which is more of a description, and
dispensable. "Ri.Hampoli," in Davenport's hand, could be
mentioned, though it has no independent authority, since it
may be wise with this work to say "Sometimes wrongly attributed
to Richard Rolle."

I have already said something about description of the
structure and about defects. Another useful piece of information which could go on sheet A or B, one suggested by Professor
Robbins in his article "Mirth in Manuscripts,"[21] is the approximate length, particularly for unidentified or unedited
items, to help people engaged on quests for either; it can
also serve as a check on the completeness of copies of better-
known texts. As the size of leaves and of writing vary so
widely, only a word estimate will be precise enough, but that
does not take too long to calculate from a total of pages or
columns and portions thereof, averages for lines and words,
and some allowance for irregularities.

More will need to be said here, on sheet B, about the subject matter of unidentified or unedited items, not only for
the benefit of users of the handlists but also for that of the
final indexers. I do not see any simple way to standardize
the mode of description of subjects or genres except by issuing
our own thesaurus of terms and/or asking contributors to relate
items to the not very satisfactory categories of the *Manual of
the Writings in Middle English*, a work which in any case we
cannot do without consulting and citing either positively or
negatively if the Handlists are to play an incidental part in
supplementing and correcting it, which I would argue will be
one of their most valuable services. Internal evidence or
external information concerning date and place of composition
or translation, purpose, readership, and so on will presumably
be summarized when not available in such bibliographical citations, along with any certain or likely source of a translation or extract.[22]

For the citation of bibliographical manuals, editions, and
studies we need both a code of conventions and directions as
to the extent to which we should abstract information from our
references about the item and manuscript in hand and other
copies of the text. Once the initial *Index of Middle English
Prose in Print* has been published, cross-reference to it and
employment of the same system of shortened citations will make
for considerable economy in the Handlists, and it may be hoped
that its citation list, first of all, and then even its entries
in draft or proof, might be made available to all collaborators
at the earliest opportunities. In the Handlists it should of
course be indicated whether an edition or study is based on or
utilizes the manuscript being recorded, or if it or any other
copy known to the reporter is ignored in the printed literature.

Substantial agreements or divergences between the manuscript
in hand and others which may be available in print or otherwise,
on a more or less curcory collation, deserve mention, but we
must expect some collaborators to be able to do more than others
in this respect, depending on their experience, time, and re-
sources. But an issue left unresolved at York is: is the *Index
of Middle English Prose in Print* to embrace and should not any-
way the Handlists include reference to all the unpublished dissertations in which alone many texts and studies are to be
found, and for the most part now fairly accessible? The *Doctrine of the Heart*, in Cosin V.III.24, is an example.[23] If
the initial *Index of Middle English Prose in Print* were to be
of Middle English prose in print and thesis, it would save
much repetition, and perhaps some ignorance, in the Handlists.

We now come, with sheet C, to some of the trickiest problems. It was generally agreed at York and embodied in the
"Guide" that we ought to provide notes of the dates of manuscripts. This is, I scarcely need to insist, the date of the
copying of the item being recorded. It may have been copied by
more than one hand, or copied by one and corrected by another,
perhaps with a lapse of time between. Convergent or divergent
opinions may be found in published scholarship, obtained from
palaeographical and art history pundits, or risked by the reporter him- or herself. There are also watermarks in paper,
and a rapidly improving literature and expertise with technical
aids for dating their use; we can at least record their presence
and approximate likenesses (in Briquet, Heawood, etc.), to
promote this aid we need.[24] If the item in question is in-
tegrally connected, the remainder of the manuscript may afford
explicit or circumstantial evidence for dating it, and this
is another reason why it is important to determine, if possible,
where scribes change; when they show symptoms of widely different times, places, or exemplars; and, besides, if such
changes coincide with quire ends or anomalies. I do not dare
to go on to propose that everyone attempt to describe the
characteristics of the handwritings employed, unless this seems
particularly relevant to the form of the text or the date; I
suspect it is still beyond such a large team to do consistently.[25]

For giving dates estimated by palaeography or art history
I doubt that we can do better than Dr. Neil Ker's formulae, a
small roman numeral for the century, qualified by *in(eunte)*,
med(io), *ex(eunte)*, with an oblique stroke between alternative
adjacent periods and a dash for work stretching over more than
one. A half-century may be indicated by a superior 1 or 2
(e.g., s. xv[1]). A scribe's hand could change very little over
a third of a century, and styles of writing sometimes persisted
much longer, though I must admit to venturing increasingly into

quarter-centuries. To any such guess we should attach the
name of its author, alive or dead. If more precise terms are
proferred, as may be possible from internal evidence or watermarks, a summary of the arguments is desirable.[26]

For the other major problem I quote the "Guide": "If it is
possible to localize the language of the manuscript, feel free
to add a note on that." This is realistically permissive, if
one can add "or origin," as the two, and the kinds of evidence
for them, are not always the same. As with dating, there is a
range of possible precision and authority in language localiza-
tion. You can quote editors and other previous scholars, try
to do it yourself by the light of the work of S. Moore, S.B.
Meech, and H. Whitehall (in *Essays and Studies in English and
Comparative Literature*, 13 [Folcroft, Pa., 1935], pp. 1-60),
crib or beg a diagnosis from those at work on the as yet unpublished Middle English Dialect Survey. Whether the latter would
be willing to provide copies of their questionnaire or a mini-
kit in the hope of culling more grist for their mill, or just
out of the kindness of their hearts, I don't know.[27] Collaboration with them seems to me, from my own experience of exchanges
with them, to be one of the opportunities of our handlisting
not to be missed, and closely linked with the interests of our
contributors and of future users. Nevertheless, in most instances it may not be possible to say very much under this
head, for want either of evidence or of time. As one less wise
in that field, I will only remind you that it will inevitably
involve discrimination between one scribe and another.

What else? Dr. Kathleen Scott, one of our Contributing
Editors, has suggested the inclusion of information about manuscripts containing pictures, painted borders, or elaborate
initials. I think it is highly relevant to our own purposes
and easy to record the presence of illustrations for our items,
or spaces left for them (sometimes filled at a later date).
To *describe* them or pure decoration would be a much larger task,
like the nomenclature of script. A detail I myself would welcome (despite a puzzling footnote of Professor Robbins[28]) is
the *dicta probatoria*, the first two words on the original
second leaf of any item which opens a volume or a quire which
may once have stood first or separately, serving to identify
it in a medieval catalog or testament. I don't think we can
record fully the evidence for the medieval, let alone the post-
medieval, ownership of every manuscript we handle, but I hope
few of us will be inclined to overlook it entirely, especially
when it may be connected with our more central concerns, such
as the state of the text, its date, or provenance. It is im-
perative to read inscriptions carefully, date them cautiously,
and not interpret their implications hastily.

After all this, it may be thought that I am asking too
much. If this were to be a one- or two-person job, like the

Index of Middle English Verse and its *Supplement*, it might be
so, but, having decided that the methods employed there will
not do for the prose, and that separate collaborators would
be responsible for different collections of manuscripts in our
second stage, then we shall be obliged to have more extensive
guidance if we are to produce Handlists of comparably high
standards and sufficient uniformity to be utilized by other
contributors for the eventual cumulative indexes. If we consider the Handlists as not merely necessary steps to that end,
but also as independent efforts able to stand on their own
(which, for very long, or, at the worst, forever, they may
have to), and furthermore as able to provide types and quantities of information not to be incorporated in or superseded
by the final indexes, we must try to anticipate some of the
uses they may serve, and encourage their authors not to treat
them perfunctorily but to make the best they can of them.
Delay, I know only too well, is the dangerous consequence of
elaboration, yet I doubt if too stringent economy will expedite
the interest of the volunteers.

> *A.I. Doyle*
> *Durham University*

NOTES

1. The only catalogue, by Thomas Rud (1668-1733), was edited
by James Raine the elder (1791-1858), *Catalogi Veteres Librorum
Ecclesiae Cathedralis Dunelm.*, Surtees Society, 7 (London, 1838),
136-91. Its inclusion under that title and misunderstanding
of the Episcopal adjective have often caused confusion, in the
minds of outsiders, with the Dean and Chapter's (Cathedral)
Library, which has a very much larger and more important collection of manuscripts, mostly inherited from the medieval monastery.

2. Cf. A.I. Doyle, *Book Collector*, 2 (1952-53), 154-55;
and 24 (1975), 25-32.

3. Miss Lorna J. Sass and Professor Constance B. Hieatt.

4. I believe that we should observe the distinction between
the *listing* (or inventories) of items in manuscripts and the
indexing or rearranging of the results, alphabetically or in
terms of other systems, at the end of each Handlist and of the
whole project. The initial *Index of Middle English Prose in
Print* will be rightly so called, and so too the envisaged end
product, but the use of the word "index" for the project has
tended to make participants describe all the work as indexing.

Carleton Brown called his first effort *A Register of Middle English Religious and Didactic Verse*, which is what Volume I was. The distinction is not just pedantic: some confusion arose in discussions at Cambridge through its being ignored. Perhaps the project would be better styled the *Register and Index of Middle English Prose*, clearly separating the register and index from the index of prose in print.

5. The last can of course be much abbreviated in their repetition.

6. E.g., Cosin V.V.12, item 1, is "the sawter of mercy compyled & drawen by Ser Johan Cressener bacheler of [law?]," in Latin but with English rubrics, followed by other Latin prayers with English rubrics, which may merit separate mention and numeration, though likewise not indexing, before we come to "the meditacion of Jordan of the lyfe and passion of iesu criste," consisting of meditations in English and prayers in Latin, which claims full treatment, as item 3 or 4.

7. Cf. Manfred Görlach, *The South English Legendary, Gilte Legende and Golden Legende*, Braunschweiger Anglistische Arbeiten, 3 (1972), pp. 19-20.

8. Cf. F.C. Tubach, *Index Exemplorum, a Handbook of Medieval Religious Tales* (Helsinki, 1969).

9. Restricting ourselves, for example, to the nearest approximation on a typewriter keyboard: ¢, /, ., :, +, ;, ?

10. E.g., M.B. Parkes, *English Cursive Book Hands 1250-1500* (Oxford, 1969), pp. xxviii-xxx; Records of Early English Drama, *Guidelines for Transcription* (Toronto, 1976).

11. See Angus McIntosh, "Towards an Inventory of Middle English Scribes," *Neuphilologische Mitteilungen*, 75 (1974), 608-09; Michael Benskin, "Local Archives and Middle English Dialects," *Journal of the Society of Archivists*, 5 (1977), 506-07 n. 9.

12. See note 10 above and cf. Helmut Gneuss, *Guide to the Editing and Preparation of Texts for the Dictionary of Old English* (Toronto, [1971]), pp. 15-16.

13. E.g., at the end of item 3, f. 150, "þat ȝe all at þe laste mowe come thedyr where ȝour owyn [*corrected to* holy] cosonys to [*corrected to* ben] aungelys ther to seen the virgyn of vyrgynys...." The corrections agree with Fitzwilliam Museum, Cambridge, McClean 132, the base for the edition by J.J. Vaissier, *A Deuout Treatyse Called the Tree & XII Frutes of the Holy Goost* (Groningen, 1960).

14. M.F. Wakelin, "The Manuscripts of John Mirk's Festial," *Leeds Studies in English*, n.s. 1 (1967), 112, says there is no prologue in the Cosin manuscript.

15. See above, p. 27.

16. See Walter Hilton, *The Goad of Love*, ed. C. Kirchberger (London, 1952), pp. 19-20; J.E. Krochalis, "*Contemplations of the Dread and Love of God*: Two Newly Identified Pennsylvania Manuscripts," *The Library Chronicle*, 42 (1977), 1-22.

17. That it has no specific address, dating clause, or signatory and that it is on a leaf integral to a quire in the middle of the volume, and written in a set hand, suggests that the purposes were more than documentary, although the content may apply to the actual context.

18. Original or early marginalia, which may supply such citations (and may need to be completed or corrected), can be incorporated in the transcriptions of beginnings and endings by the use of round (and, where altered, square) brackets. The occurrence of these and other marginalia may be noted on sheet B.

19. See p. 69 above: the sixty-five articles of the *Meditationes de Passione* by Jordan of Saxony (von Quedlinburg) are common in continental copies, though known to me in only this one Middle English prose rendering apart from a lost early sixteenth-century printed edition and a derivative.

20. The list of copies from the University of London M.A. thesis (1962) by Clare Goymer is unfortunately far from comprehensive. Professor N.F. Blake is at work on a fuller study and edition.

21. R.H. Robbins, "Mirth in Manuscripts," *Essays & Studies*, n.s. 21 (1968), 15-28.

22. For example, the legend of St. Barbara in Cosin V.IV.4 is a translation from the Latin of Jan van Wackerzele, an identification I owe to Mrs. Margaret Crane.

23. Edited by Mary P. Candon; see *Dissertation Abstracts*, 24 (1964), 4173.

24. See, for instance, Allan Stevenson, "Paper as Bibliographical Evidence," *The Library*, 5th series, 17 (1962), 197-212; "The Quincentennial of Netherlandish Bookblocks," *British Museum Quarterly*, 31 (1966), 83-87; and his revised edition of C.M. Briquet, *Les Filigranes* (Amsterdam, 1968), especially I, *15-*36. The Bodleian Library now offers a regular service of beta-radiographic prints of watermarks in its collections, with

the aid of a growing reference file to existing negatives.
Other British libraries have facilities, and Professor Stephen
Spector, Department of English, State University of New York at
Stony Brook, plans to produce a catalogue of dated specimens
from United States libraries.

25. A pessimism produced by some of the early effects of
my own Special Lectures at King's College, London, on "Later
Middle English Manuscripts," 1965, and of M.B. Parkes' *English
Cursive Book Hands*, but the latter is perhaps now beginning to
be better understood and applied. The tentative format for
machine processing of the present project offered by Dr. Anthony
Martin to the Cambridge Conference included an optional slot
for such a characterization.

26. E.g., Cosin V.II.14 not before Sept. 1, 1429 ("Anno
VIIIo H.VIti," f. 97v), probably after 1460 (approximate composition of B. Burgh's *Cato*), i.e., s. xv ex.; Cosin V.III.9
between Dec. 1419 or 1421 (internal allusions) and Feb. 11,
1426 (last record of Hoccleve alive); Cosin V.IV.2 signed by
Thomas Olyphauntt Capellanus 1477 (f. 89v as owner, 116v as
scribe, July 12); Cosin V.V.12 not before 1495 (f. 2r), i.e.,
s. xv ex./xvi in.

27. Professor McIntosh, co-Director of the Middle English
Dialect Survey, of the Department of English Language, University of Edinburgh, did distribute at the Conference copies of
his questionnaire for the preliminary analysis of Middle
English dialects, and generously offered to provide reports on
the results to all Contributing Editors who completed them.

28. "Mirth in Manuscripts," p. 28 n. 94.

COLLECTION, CALL NO., & ITEM NO.

TITLE(S), AUTHORSHIP, CONTENT, DIVISIONS, LENGTH, DEFECTS

EDITIONS, STUDIES, CITATIONS, & OTHER MSS (above or over)

[Sheet B]

LOCALITY

LIBRARY

COLLECTION & CALL NO.

CATALOGUE REFERENCE(S)

ITEM NO.   BEGINNING ON FOLIO/PAGE

ENDING ON FOLIO/PAGE
(above or over)

[Sheet A]

COLLECTION, CALL NO., & ITEM NO.
SCRIBE(S), CORRECTOR(S), ANNOTATOR(S), DATING, & PLACING

WATERMARKS, ILLUSTRATIONS, DICTA PROBATORIA, ETC.
(above or over)
[Sheet C]

SOME PROBLEMS OF IDENTITY
AND IDENTIFICATION IN
WYCLIFFITE WRITINGS

> I met a man upon the stair,
> And when I looked he was not there;
> He was not there again today--
> I wish to God he'd go away!

Anyone who works for even a short time on Wycliffite writings is likely to give heartfelt sympathy to the speaker in Mearns' poem (here in the version corrupted by oral transmission). How often have I read through a manuscript in a library and thought, "I have read that before"; and then, when I have scratched through my notes to find the passage, I have gone back to the manuscript only to discover that though similar, it is not quite the same. Yet on a third look the same familiarity recurs; where *was* that wretched passage? Or, to take another problem to which the ditty is equally appropriate, how often have I read through a set of sermons or a tract and felt, by the itching of my palms, that a Lollard wrote them; yet, trying to isolate anything that could be regarded as decisively Wycliffite, I have had to admit that the text could be just radically orthodox. The problem here is rather different: that there was a spectrum of opinion ranging from that of such ardent defenders of the establishment as archbishop Arundel or the Carmelite Thomas Netter to the extremes of Lollardy that went far beyond Wyclif himself, but that in the center was a large grey area where the authors at best did not wish to define their position, and at worst did not understand the issues sufficiently clearly to be able to do so. To expect writing on ecclesiastical issues around 1410-30 *not* to reflect Wycliffite thinking is as naive as to think that any sociological writing of the second half of this century can fail to reflect the thought of Marx or Freud.

For the *Index of Middle English Prose*, however, the problems met in placing texts within or outside the range of Lollard authorship are not important. Any categorization of type should, I think, keep to a genre description and not extend to an attempt to define the ideas within the work. I want

briefly now to look at my first problem and to indicate some
of the main ways in which it is bound to affect the *Index*.
Ideas as such do not concern the *Index*; form is much more important. I do not pretend in what follows that the problems
I shall discuss are peculiar to Wycliffite texts; they are
bound to recur in many other fields where prose is being used
not for an autonomous work of art but for the imparting of
information or for persuasion towards a view--wherever, in
short, the medium is *not* the message. But Wycliffite texts
provide some good examples.

Before going on to these examples, however, it is perhaps
right to raise some basic questions. Most vitally, what do we
expect the *Index* to provide when complete? Ideally, I suppose,
and most simply, a list of all the known manuscripts of a given
work; the *Index* should make it possible to look up, under its
incipit, a work, say the Wycliffite Bible or the *Lanterne of
Liȝt*, and find a series of press marks which will enable us to
know how many manuscripts survive and where they are located.
The incipient editor will thus know the scope of his project,
and will be saved from the nightmare that he may find another
manuscript the week before his edition is published or his
thesis examined. The literary critic will be able to assess
the popularity of the work at issue and, with more labor, the
milieu in which it circulated. But how realistic is the ideal
from which all these desirable blessings flow? With the
Ancrene Riwle, or even with Rolle, the problems are small;
the works have been published and are relatively familiar,
and the indexer can be expected to recognize them. In other,
less well-charted areas of religious prose there is much more
difficulty. My choice of examples above was deliberate, though
hardly deeply studied. While the *Lanterne of Liȝt* survives,
or more properly is *known* to survive, in only two manuscripts
and an early printed edition in all of which it was transcribed
without modification or omission,[1] and is hence easily identifiable, the Wycliffite Bible presents much more serious problems. In the first place the number of manuscripts already
known is much greater, some 250 in all.[2] Secondly, many of
these do not contain more than a small part of the translation.
While it may be easy to describe briefly those that contain,
for instance, just the New Testament or even smaller units
such as a complete book, what is to be done in the *Index* about
the manuscripts that contain extracts or summaries of the translation? A fair example of this would be John Rylands Manchester
English 83. Here the translation of Proverbs is followed by
the heading "here suen a fewe tixtis of Ecclesiastes"; eight
folios later we are promised the first nine chapters of Wisdom,
and there is then a part of the sixteenth chapter, followed by
a summary, becoming increasingly brief, of Ecclesiasticus; the

manuscript ends with eight folios of pious texts, some biblical, some patristic, some whose sources are not stated. The
third problem of the Bible translation is, of course, that of
version. It would be a work of extreme labor to discover
whether, for instance, the summaries in Rylands English 83
derive from the Later Version, like the translation of the
opening chapters of Wisdom, even if, indeed, any conclusion
could be drawn from such abbreviated versions. The mind bog-
gles at the equipment an indexer would need to determine such
matters. I would suggest that this third problem falls outside
the business of the *Index*; but the second poses more of a
dilemma. Is it best, because quicker, to take the line that a
rough description is sufficient (say, for Rylands English 83,
just "summary of material from Wisdom and Ecclesiasticus,
followed by pious texts")? It might be argued that there are
not, after all, such a large number of different Middle English
biblical translations outside sermons, and the scholar concerned
with the area can pursue the matter further. Or should the
wretched indexer be told to define precisely the passages ren-
dered, even when this results in a long list of references to
describe an idiosyncratic manuscript that may have no partner
in its crime? My own view would be that the latter course of
action is impossibly cumbersome, and that the *Index* will never
appear if it is followed. But a failure to scrutinize what
may at first sight appear as biblical translation of an idiosyncratic kind can easily lead to confusion of the issue, and
a confusion of exactly the kind that the *Index* must strive, if
it is to be of any use, to avoid. I myself was misled by the
headings in the second half of Huntington HM 501 into thinking
that the material was a series of extracts from the Wycliffite
New Testament. Professor Ralph Hanna put me right, correctly
identifying the text as the opening of the English version of
Clement of Llanthony's *Harmony of the Gospels*, without the
prefatory material or usual headings and with the marginal
rubrics of a manuscript such as B.L. Royal 17.C.xxxiii used as
main headings. The difficulty for the indexer here would be
that Clement of Llanthony in its English version has not been
printed, and its variant forms are therefore much less well
known than those of the Wycliffite Bible.

Turning to other problems for the *Index*, my first example
concerns a text that I have briefly discussed elsewhere.[3] In
four manuscripts is preserved a long text, purporting to be a
sermon, dealing with the good Lollard topics of the right of
the clergy to own material wealth and the mendicancy of the
friars. Despite the loss of leaves that all manuscripts save
the latest have suffered, there is no difficulty in recognizing
the text as identical in all four. It is not quite so obvious,
however, that there is considerable overlap between this text

and another found in a single manuscript at Lambeth Palace
Library. This second is a tract, not a sermon, and this results in more drastic differences than just the absence of
text and various addresses to the congregation. Its most
striking features are the ten-chapter division and an appendix
of authorities, partly in English, partly in Latin. Thinking
about the text from the viewpoint of the present *Index*, no
length of incipit, however generously drawn, would reveal the
identity of the Lambeth text with the other manuscripts. For
Lambeth takes only about the second half of the material in
the others; various sections even of that second half are ignored, while, conversely, new passages are added. I am
assuming here that Lambeth is the derivative version, and this
I believe so far to be the case, but this is not important
for the *Index*. It is for the *Index* to record, and the editor
to judge. But any editor would have to take the Lambeth text
into consideration. How can the *Index* workers hope to record
information that would allow for its identification with the
other manuscripts?

One possibility exists that would help enormously in Wycliffite texts, though it would greatly increase the laborious-
ness of the indexing work: this would be to record the citation
of any authorities, particularly if these are more precise
than just naming the author. A very common type of Lollard
text consists of a string of passages translating extracts
from the fathers, from canon law, and, less frequently, from
medieval theological writers. The *Floretum/Rosarium* and the
Glossed Gospels consist entirely of such sequences: the
Lanterne of Liȝt, the *Thirty-Seven Conclusions*, and the
Apology for Lollard Doctrines[4] are further, more familiar
texts built largely upon this method. There are also less
extensive instances where the method is used to build up a
tract designed to establish the Lollard view on such subjects
as the Eucharist, biblical translation, images, or pilgrimages.
Because the complete text lacks any artistic shape--it was
never meant to have one--and because the structure is purely
one of constant accretion, these texts are fluid in their form.
At the lowest level, some quotations are dropped while others
are added; so again no incipit or explicit will necessarily
reveal similarity or identity. At a higher level, the strings
of quotations are used as the skeleton of a more complex structure. As Dr. von Nolcken has shown, a string may be taken
into a longer sermon or tract, and the sequence of strings
may form the structural principle for a sermon.[5] The only way
in which this adaptation can possibly be recognized is if the
authorities are included in the *Index*. Yet this would vastly
increase the bulk of the finished work, and the complexity of
the operation for those working through the manuscripts. I

think that a case can be made only for recording citations where at least the work as well as the author is mentioned by name. A reference as vague as some we have all met, such as "and, as Augustine says, God is love," is of no value, but to know of a sequence of canon law citations, including division of the law, *distinctio*, chapter, and so forth, may allow one to bring together two texts whose overlap could not otherwise be spotted. Obviously this sort of laborious documentation is not needed for texts that have been studied or edited; if the indexer can recognize the work as such, then only a reference is needed.

But unfortunately even this lengthy process would not cope with all the problems, even in the Wycliffite field. To take another instance that I have also described elsewhere,[6] in C.U.L. Ii.6.26 there is a series of twelve tracts on the desirability of vernacular scripture; in the past they have been ascribed to John Purvey, though like most other works that modern critics have given to that legendary figure, they cannot be shown to have anything to do with him. In fact, several of the twelve turn up elsewhere in other guises. A particularly interesting instance in the present context is the seventh. This shares most of its material with a text known as *Pater Noster II*, printed by Arnold among the *Select English Works of Wyclif*; as its name implies, this version is a commentary on the Lord's Prayer, each clause being commented on sequentially. It is very difficult to be sure which of these two versions, tract or commentary, is the original; for the *Index*, however, originality does not matter. But if the identity of the two texts had not already been recognized, how could the *Index* have facilitated the discovery? The incipits and explicits of the two are completely different, the basic structure and the declared subjects likewise discrepant. Only one patristic authority is cited, and that only in the *Pater Noster II* in a passage not found in the Cambridge tract. Indexing biblical references might help, though the sequences would not be identical in the two versions because of omissions and additions. The only possible help might come through a summary of the contents. This, if sufficiently detailed, would reveal that the *Pater Noster II* shows a recurrent concern with the Lollard aim of making the scriptures available in the vernacular, and thus would lead the researcher on to tracts whose declared purpose is persuasion to this. But it is here, of course, that coordination of a large team of indexers becomes most difficult. It is easy enough to instruct a worker to record, say, fifty words of an incipit or explicit; it is straightforward, if rebarbative, to such a worker to be told to index authorities or even biblical references; but a summary of subject matter impinges upon the subjective and cannot be

precisely defined. The results would be far more unpredictable
and inevitably uneven. Someone summarizing *Pater Noster II*
might quite reasonably be so influenced by the dominance (rein-
forced visually by rubrication in some manuscripts) of the
prayer's clauses that the importance of the topic of translation could be lost.

Many of these problems perhaps appear in their most acute
form when one comes to sermons, Wycliffite or orthodox. It
is clear that the incipits and explicits of sermons are peculiarly open to modification: the piety of the preacher, or his
desire for rhetorical flourish, may lead to amplification of
the opening address or the final prayer; irritation or laziness
of the scribe may result in the abbreviation of these. While
the citation of a liturgically chosen text linked to its appropriate occasion may seem to fix a sermon to some extent, and
make it for that reason readily identifiable, this aid may not
be invariably efficacious. This can be shown from the large
sermon-cycle copied many times by the Lollards. In all but
one of the manuscripts that preserve the sermons on the Sunday
gospels in that cycle, each sermon is preceded by a Latin
quotation of, and reference to, a gospel text and by an occasion; these belong together according to the Sarum rite, and
the sermons that follow provide, among other things, a commentary on the passage whose opening words have been quoted. An
Index giving incipit and explicit would readily identify these
manuscripts. But another manuscript, Sidney Sussex Cambridge
74, modifies this pattern by heading each sermon with an epistle
text in Latin with the biblical reference, and by appending to
each gospel sermon, without any intervening gap, a sermon on
that epistle.[7] The explicits to the sermons are thus totally
different, and the incipits only similar, if at all, from the
opening English words and not from the headings; even here
minor rewording is not infrequent and is of a kind that could
disguise the identity of individual homilies. Because of this
sort of alteration it seems to me important that each sermon be
indexed separately; simply to index the first and last sermons
of a sequence reduces enormously the chances of identifications
being made.

The basic point involved here is, of course, the absence of
any sense of autonomy of a piece of writing and the lack of any
inhibiting sense of author's prerogative. Originality is nowhere sought. The existing work is likely to be a patchwork
of the most homely sort--one patch on top of another patch,
and darning and cobbling between the pieces that do not quite
join up. This process is evident also from an area that is
only just being studied. It has long been known that Lollard
writers took over orthodox works and introduced into them their
own heterodox views; the Pepys *Ancrene Riwle*, various redactions

of Rolle's Psalter commentary, and one version of Thoresby's *Lay Folks Catechism* are the most familiar instances. But it is now being discovered that the reverse process also happens: Lollard works were modified and adapted to more orthodox tastes. At least four instances of this process are now known with the sermon-cycle that I am engaged in editing. Again, all the obvious indexer's tools will be useless: in each, the incipits and explicits of the sermons are drastically altered; though some references remain the same, others are omitted or added; by definition the most obvious marks of subject matter, the Lollard denunciations of images, pilgrimages, oral confession, and so forth are expurgated. In one case the most obvious matter taken over from the Lollard sermons is the biblical translation of the gospel for the day, a translation that in the Lollard sermons is often spread out through the sermon but in the orthodox redaction is gathered together into an initial straightforward reading.[8] Here I think there can be no solution for the *Index*; there is no method that can allow for identification of such parallels, important though they are for the measurement of the influence of the Lollard movement.

At any rate, however, it is usually obvious when a sermon has ended, even in the written form to which the modern scholar is limited. This is by no means the case with many prose texts. The strings of authorities are perhaps the most obvious instance in the Wycliffite area. The series may start, sometimes, declaredly, as dealing with the Eucharist, but then wander off by imperceptible stages on to other related topics, images, confession, and so forth. In the Lambeth manuscript to which I referred above, is the "appendix" of authorities a separate text, or a necessary appendage? At its worst this problem can be seen in a manuscript in the British Library, Harley 3913;[9] this is a commonplace book of notes on various topics, some of them specifically with a Lollard slant, others less controversial, with quotations from authorities. The material is only occasionally divided off by headings, and these vary from the vaguest (such as "De homine") to the more specific (such as "Contra questores"). Much of this particular manuscript is Latin, but others of this kind where all is in English are bound to be the bane of the life of the wretched indexer who is obliged to describe them.

Having looked at a few of the many problems, are there any suggestions for solutions? Solutions are not easy to find, but a few constraints seem to me important to accept. In the first and most important place, it appears to me absolutely essential that it should be accepted that the *Index* must be provisional--accepted by both those working towards its production and by those who will eventually use it. The work of the indexer cannot be a substitute for the work of the editor.

Classification of all kinds, and the identification of one
piece with another, must, save in the most obvious cases, be
the responsibility of the editor. The *Index* should aim to
alert the editor, but not to define his area of vision. If
the *Index* aims at complete identification, it will never be
finished; if it does not accept its extreme provisionality,
we ourselves shall never gain any benefit from it. On the
other hand, it seems important to stress the need, at least
in the Handlists of manuscripts, for completeness--that no
scrap, however apparently insignificant, should be ignored.
The first twenty-five folios of Camb. Trinity B.14.50 were
not mentioned by the various scholars who had previously
worked on the Wycliffite contents of the remainder; it is easy
to see why, since they are, apparently, just notes for sermons.
But those notes refer to the *Rosarium* and provide important
evidence that that alphabetical set of *distinctiones* was indeed
used in the construction of Lollard homilies by an English
preacher. It is equally desirable that any possible division
within a manuscript should be noted, in case this will facilitate the recognition that part of the contents are to be found
elsewhere. Yet it must be accepted that in a few cases listing
of incipits and explicits of all pieces may have to be aban-
doned, since a full listing, with fifty words of each, would
result in transcribing the whole manuscript. When the indexer
is faced with what is plainly a notebook, the only realistic
answer seems to be to list briefly the subjects that appear
to dominate. From the point of view of my own area of interest,
I would hope that some method could be used to indicate the
presence of Latin items in a manuscript, though a full description would obviously be outside the scope of the *Index*. Others
can doubtless contribute similar requests, and it must be accepted that only a brief signal and not a complete account can
be realistic.

     Finally, there is one further point about the provisional
nature of the *Index* that needs stressing. Instinctively, and
it is apparently an instinct that is shared, we feel that to
index prose is more difficult than to index verse. There is,
of course, more prose than verse; incipits and explicits seem
less fixed, and, lacking the constraints of rhyme and metre,
interpolation and extraction is simpler in prose. To some extent all this is true. But it is easy to forget the cross-
references and notes in Rossell Hope Robbins' *Index of Middle
English Verse* that make evident that all these problems arose
there. But for the *Index of Middle English Prose* we have not
the advantage of a cumulative memory; there will be many indexers, not just two. This will impose limitations on the
eventual publications, but also suggests conditions that need
to be observed in the accumulation of material: over-copiousness,

the willingness to send and to answer queries, the readiness
to revise a description, even perhaps the use of a signal for
a manuscript that is peculiarly recalcitrant of summary. And
we must face the fact that even when all the parts are available,
we shall still be scratching our heads and muttering, "I've
read that before, but where in heaven's name was it?"--and
finding no easy answer in the *Index*.

Anne Hudson
Oxford University

NOTES

1. B.L. Harley 2324 was used as the basis of the only modern
edition, that by L.M. Swinburn (EETS, o.s. 151 [1917]); Harley
6613 also contains the text, though some leaves are now missing.
The text was printed by Redman around 1530 (STC 15225).

2. The texts were printed by J. Forshall and F. Madden
(Oxford, 1850), 4 vols.; more recently a fuller list of manuscripts was printed by C. Lindberg, *Studia Neophilologica*, 42
(1970), 333-47, but additions can still be made to this.

3. See *Selections from English Wycliffite Writings* (Cambridge, 1978), pp. 185-86; a complete edition of this text is
in preparation.

4. The *Apology* was edited by J.H. Todd (Camden Society,
1842); some details about the *Glossed Gospels* and *Conclusions*,
together with further bibliography, are available in *Selections*,
pp. 166-68, 170-71, 198-99, and for the *Floretum/Rosarium* in
Journal of Theological Studies, n.s. 22 (1972), 65-81.

5. Selections from the English version of the *Rosarium*,
with introductory discussion by Christina von Nolcken, will be
published shortly in the Heidelberg series of Middle English
texts.

6. See *Selections*, pp. 189-91.

7. The sermons as they appear in the majority of manuscripts
were printed by T. Arnold, *Select English Works of John Wyclif*
(Oxford, 1869-71), I, 1-162; the variant manuscript was described in E.W. Talbert, "A Fifteenth-Century Lollard Sermon
Cycle," *University of Texas Studies in English* (1939), 5-30.

8. These derivatives will be discussed in my forthcoming
edition of the sermons; the most extensive use of them is in
a set of sermons found in Dublin Trinity C.1.22, and in part

in Camb. St. John's G.22 and C.U.L. Add. 5338.

     9. I owe knowledge of this to the generosity of Dr. A.I. Doyle.

SOME PROBLEMS IN INDEXING
MIDDLE ENGLISH RECIPES

My title is "Some problems in indexing Middle English
recipes," but I shall in fact be concerned only with medical
recipes, of which in all conscience there are enough. General
recipes--how to make all apples fall from a tree,[1] how to take
birds--and magical ones--how to make a dog seem dead, how to
make fire go out of a vessel full of water[2]--I have glanced
at and occasionally made note of; culinary recipes--how to
dight a swan--I have looked at with watering mouth but made
no effort to list or compare;[3] farriery recipes I have simply
put aside. There were enough unpleasant concoctions "For the
man that may not piss" for me not to want to go on to those
"For the horse that may not piss." But doubtless the lessons
and methods we learn from medical recipes can be applied to
other groups.

My interest in Middle English medical recipes started from
one of our own manuscripts in Aberdeen University Library, MS
258, a late fifteenth-century manuscript which contains only
herbal and medical material. M.R. James noted that there was
a great deal of repetition in it; just how much he did not
investigate,[4] but it is still unique in my experience in that
it contains five copies of the same herbal text, *The Virtues
of Herbs*, each followed by a collection of recipes. All is in
one handwriting, item follows item on the same page, and the
original quiring proves that the manuscript was designed to
take its present shape; there is no question of the loose
papers on the scriptorium tables having been swept up at the
end of the day and bound together by mistake. Intermittently
over the last ten years I have been tracing further copies of
The Virtues of Herbs and have extended my search to the
recipes. I have, I suppose, handled over two hundred manuscripts (which is nowhere near the total available even in
readily accessible libraries) containing this sort of material,
though I would not claim to have examined them all systematically; when time has pressed, especially in the earlier years, I
have tended to concentrate on *The Virtues of Herbs* rather than

the recipes. But apart from a few such scholars as R.H. Robbins, whose paper "Medical Manuscripts in Middle English" has
been a regular standby,[5] and C.H. Talbot of the Wellcome Insti-
tute for the History of Medicine, I suppose I have looked at
more Middle English medical recipes, certainly recently, than
most people. There is little for congratulation in this and
a great deal for commiseration. These recipes have, of course,
not the slightest scintilla of literary interest. Detailed
findings from their examination may well cast light on various
aspects of social history--the organization of the cheap book
trade perhaps, the history of medicine certainly--but the in-
tellectual problems they produce at the initial stage are essentially those of classification and arrangement, of establishing
relationships. This is ample justification for posing some of
the problems to a group that is starting to index all Middle
English prose.

What, first and foremost, are we going to take as the unit
to index? The individual recipe? Most of them have a standard
form, with a title, be it in Latin or English, and a text. The
titles are often distinctive: "For clensyng of þe hede," "A
good oynement for vanite of the hede," "A precious water for to
clarifye þe eyen & do away þe perle ore þe hawe"; but title and
text together would often fall considerably short of the fifty
words of text, excluding titles, that our draft instructions[6]
recommend as the minimum that we should transcribe from each
text. To take the recipe as the unit would therefore involve
transcribing virtually all the text, and the corpus of recipes
would clog up the filing cabinets and later dominate the whole
Index. And this would not be the only difficulty.

Sooner or later, when the *Index* passes from the stage of
manuscript indexes to first-line indexes, someone will have to
decide what degree of identity is necessary to justify including
two variants under a common head. What would he do with the
series to which I have given the working heading "Forty
variants" of the recipe for which the title is "For clensyng
of þe hede" or "For purging of þe hede"? There is evidence
of scribal miscopying in *þe licor* (7), *festeryng* (31) and *seþe*
(24); there is a line introduced by mistake from another recipe
in (40), found also in a Yale manuscript; there is a good deal
of synonym substitution: *take* (1), *nym* (28); *clense* (10),
purge (1), *spurge* (14, 19); *ache* (1), *achyng* (22, 31), *warke*
(25), *warking* (16), *payne* (12); *do away* (1), *put awaye* (18),
bynymen (25), *fordo* (32). Some variants show simplification
by omission, from *peletre of spayne* to *peletre* (19), from three
specified benefits in (1) to two (23, 24) to one (35) to none
(37, 38); or confusions of word order (4, 15) or amplifications,
whether stock ones (9, 37) common to many recipes or more
specific ones (5, 6, 16, 29, 35). No one, seeing the forty put

together as they are, can doubt that they are "the same" recipe; but it would be a bold editor who would recognize (39) and (40) as such without the other thirty-eight.

This is perhaps an extreme case; the recipe happens to be one that I chose for sampling at an early stage and so have collected the most specimens of. But to a somewhat lesser extent, variation can be observed in all these recipes, as Margaret Ogden and others have noticed.[7] On the reasons for it one can only speculate. Some element of scribal miscopying there must be, but this cannot account for all variation. Did some scribes write virtually from memory texts that, in a commercial scriptorium, they might have to reproduce several times a day? Did some, acting as editors, try to give the "guts" of the recipe in their exemplar in an attempt to produce a shorter and presumably therefore a cheaper version? Is there reason to suspect some element of retranslation from Latin or from French and Latin? Many of the medical manuscripts of Middle English are written in a mixture of languages, and occasionally one gets such versions as:

Pro gutta calida bonum unguentum R erbiue playnteyne henbane þe flowre of brom howselek endyue j red rose vel melius white roses quia isti plus sunt frigidi & ideo meliores j violet sed modicum heyrewe & walworte sed modicum & maybotur & olye & suet de deer & marye de equis & merye de net bonis & grece de pedibus neet & grece de capitibus om[i]nis & gryce de bawsoun sed modicum quia calidum est olibanum & cera alba & j morel þe jus quia hoc optime valet R centorie puluer & bibe in cervisia antiqua & valet optime pro stomaco & idem faciet hominem habere appetitum ad comedendum & valet pro homine þat may nawghte browkyn no mete.

(Cosin V:III:11, f. 30ᵛ)

which in their macaronic effect produce as it were a gross caricature of some Middle English lyrics.

Certainly the practical difficulties at both the first and the second stage would seem to rule out the feasibility of indexing each recipe independently. There are other possible courses. One would be to omit the recipes altogether from the *Index*, thus treating them like "anything that can loosely be called a legal document--statutes, muniments, deeds, wills etc.," or like "lists or inventories, accounts and so on"--to quote our draft instructions again. Since the *Index* is not attempting to list the source material for administrative, legal or economic history, it could be argued, why should it concern itself with the source material for a minor branch of social history? There would be consequences for the lexicographer and

the historian of syntax in his having no references readily
available to sources of potentially relevant material, but the
same consequences are going to operate with material of legal
interest anyhow.

For casual or isolated recipes this might be an appropriate
course of action, and of these Robbins has reminded us that
"hundreds ... are found scribbled on unused fly-leaves in almost every kind of manuscript."[8] Everyone who has handled
manuscripts knows how often such casual waifs turn up. But
the recipes tend to accumulate into collections of half a dozen
recipes or half a dozen pages. Larger collections again,
though essentially of the same nature, are frequently arranged
and numbered systematically, with an index preceding or following them. It is hard to see how such collections could properly
be excluded from the *Index*, especially as on occasions they
are given a formal unity by the addition of a preface too long
to be treated as a title alone. Thus Sloane 2581, f. 5, introduces a collection to be listed below not only with a much
elaborated form, over one hundred words long, of the "Galen,
Asclepius and Ipocras" title, but with a further preface,
"First as of a congruens it is most expedient in euery werke
begunne to shewe thoru small cause how and be what means euery
thing and most especiall this present worke ... drawith his
originall...." The final stage is reached when recipes are
closely integrated into a systematic medical treatise, like
those in Guy of Chauliac's *Surgery*, and so become a part of a
larger text.[9] No indexer would for a moment dream of leaving
out such texts from the *Index*; but where, in a continuum of
this kind, do we draw the line, to include some and exclude
others? If we were to think of omitting recipes from the main
index but including them in a *Corpus Medicamentorum*, the same
difficulty, of where to draw the line, would arise, complicated
by that raised when we thought of indexing by recipes, for if a
Corpus Medicamentorum is to have any value, it too must be comprehensive, and its compilation would necessitate the recording
and comparison of individual recipes.

But perhaps we are really standing on our head in talking
of casual recipes being "accumulated" into collections; should
we not rather be thinking of a starting point of formal collections, derived I suspect ultimately from classical sources,
representing translations of contemporary Latin collections,
with the most popular elements being extracted and copied independently, to give the casual fly-leaf recipes? We should
then have to adopt the collection as the indexing unit, and
surely we ought to be encouraged to do so by the knowledge
that the informing principle generally in Latin and French
as well as in English collections seems to be to proceed *de
capite ad pedem*. Classification of recipes "For head-ache"

should therefore go some way to enable us to see how far this principle will carry us. In the list in the Appendix headed "Twenty-five Recipes" are presented the most frequently used recipes I have identified in my notes[10]--though here I would remind you that this is very much an interim report. Within the twenty-five are two that have turned up only once each (W, Y); the number of times each of the others occurs is given by the figure at the left of the foot of each recipe. You will notice that B is the most common, but please remember that since I was using it as a test specimen I was specifically looking for it. D is separated into three versions because of the difference in the opening words but also because one of these versions frequently starts a collection. In view of the evidence of the "Forty Variants" it might be argued that D is a variant of A no more extreme than 39 is of 1; but I assume a clear distinguishing mark in the presence of the word "lye." In the same way Z may be claimed as a distant variant of C, though they cannot be linked (at least, they cannot be linked by me) through a chain of intermediate stages; the number of ingredients differs, and C is common, Z is rare, so I have left them as separate. The accompanying list of "Some Opening Orders" shows the occurrence of these twenty-five as the first three elements in various collections; it also takes account of the presence of *Index of Middle English Verse* 3422, "The man that wole...," and of the title given by Robbins from Harley 2378, p. 229, as:

> Here begynnyth medicynis þat good lechis haue made and
> drawyn out of hir bokys, Galien, Asclipius and Ipocras.
> Þes were the beste lechis of the world, of al maner
> sorys and woundys, cancrys, gowtys, festrys, felons,
> and for sodeyn sorys and al maner iuelys in the body,
> within and withoute.

Already some general observations can be made: though the symbol "?" occurs once (and, with more accurate notetaking on my part, would not have occurred at all), the symbol "X," left to cater for hitherto-unlisted headache recipes, is not in fact called into use. Other recipes for headache are there, but they have not turned up in my opening orders. Further: for about five out of every six collections, the likeliest start is A or D; orders beginning A are more stable than those beginning D; whereas the presence of *Index of Middle English Verse* 3422 as an introduction is usually a strong indication that the following collection will begin ABC or xABC, no such generalization can be made about the Galen title. Though the list suggests that a variant of D is most likely to follow it, Ashmole 7706 follows it with "A good leteway for alle maner couȝynge."

This seems to me to be leading towards a system of classification which is neither impossibly complicated nor gravely
out of step with the methods and instructions already established. Any indexer who transcribed at least fifty words of
the text would fairly often transcribe in the process enough
of the third recipe, especially in those collections where
this is crucial, to ensure its identification at a later stage.
He would not do so, of course, in collections beginning with A,
but if his instructions were modified to "Transcribe at least
fifty words, including the first ten or twelve of each of the
first three recipes," he should then be able to provide enough
evidence to facilitate at least an umambiguous identification
of the opening of the collection. At the end of the text,
transcription of the concluding lines would need to be accom-
panied by some indication of the recipe in which they occur,
for which the title ought to be adequate, but more of this
anon. And it would be most necessary also to give some indication of the approximate number of recipes in the collection.
Approximate the number would have to be, for though in most
collections there is clear indication, by titles, rubrication,
underlining, paragraphing or marginal mark, that a new recipe
is beginning, scribes differ widely in how they present a suc-
cession of recipes for the same ailment. Sometimes they indicate each one fully, underlining or rubricating such a title
as "Another," "For the same," "Alia." Sometimes they run two
or three together, especially the shorter ones, omitting the
intermediate "Another" or replacing it by a simple "or". This
uncertainty obtains even when the recipes are numbered and indexed.
    If these fairly minor modifications to the draft instruc-
tions are made, it should be possible with little more effort
than for other texts to identify collections likely to be
standard and provide at least the sort of basis for further
detailed investigation of relationships that the *Index of Middle
English Verse* provides for lyrics. A specimen entry might well
read rather like this:

Aberdeen U.L. 258

p. 167   Make lye of varuayne oþer of bytayne oþer of
wormod and þerwyt wasshe þin hed þries in þe woke.
Anoþer þyng for þe heed   Take peletre of spayne and chewe
þe rote iij dayes ... a good drinke for þe heed   Take
bytonye and veruayne and wormod and celondoyne &
waybrode....

... and þan goo ly doun on þi bed and wrye þe warme and
take a good slepe.

A collection of about 145 recipes, ending in "Anoþer for
þe same [þe accys] whanne þin accys ys passyd"

which is close enough to the specimen entry provided in our instructions to make its initial preparation and subsequent handling possible by whatever procedures are generally adopted. There would, however, still be many obstacles.

Collections imperfect at beginning or end would provide a particular difficulty. It is one that our organizers must already have faced and drafted some solutions for in general terms. With recipes, however--probably because, as practical aids to leech-craft, they remained in use when more literary works, and especially more devotional works, had fallen out of fashion--the number of imperfect, dog-eared, and generally scruffy manuscripts is greater, in my experience, than in other areas. Hans Sloane and Elias Ashmole preserved many paper manuscripts for us; they also rebound large numbers of them, tidying them up and shedding leaves in the process. Sometimes there is some indication of the number in the collection attached to the first preserved recipe; otherwise familiarity with standard collections may enable an indexer to identify some of the material, but the number of acephalous entries is likely to be high. And just where the end of a collection of recipes falls is often difficult to determine; I give in my specimen with great show of confidence the details for the collection in Aberdeen U.L. 258, p. 167. I now confess that for no other collection in this manuscript could I be so confident that I had identified the last recipe. For a collection beginning ABC on page 207, which is numbered and which therefore I have been in the habit of using as a standard list, there are two recipes in Latin following the last of the numbered ones, and then two more in English without titles. All is in the same handwriting; what is to be regarded as the end of the collection? Similarly with the list beginning AST on page 273. After some 234 recipes or rubricated English titles, the last English, in a recipe "Pro sicco scabbe," reads "...& clense hem togedur & drynke it erliche & late ix dayes." It goes on, "Item pro eodem unguatur unguento salso in palmis & in plantis pedum ad quantitatem pise mane & sero & delebitur scabies siccus. Liber de diversis aquis...;" and into a series of Latin recipes for waters, paralleled elsewhere, and concluding in English with a list of the virtues of nutmeg. Where does this collection end? With the last recipe whose title as well as text is in English, since this is the basis of most entries? With the one whose title is in Latin, text in English? With the one whose title and whose text are both in Latin? With the Latin waters? Or with the English nutmeg? An indexer, perhaps inexperienced in the special problems, has to decide fairly quickly: and his spot decision will facilitate or complicate identification at a later stage.

As difficult as incomplete manuscripts, but far less easily recognizable, are those where genuine recipes are mixed up with

closely related material which is still not quite a recipe.
Again from Aberdeen U.L. 258, here are two instances. The
fourth copy of *The Virtues of Herbs* begins with its usual
title, "Here men may see þe vertuis of herbes whiche been
hoot and whiche been cold and for how many þinges þay are
good." It goes on in one of its usual orders to page 140,
where in the middle of a sentence in "mynte" it breaks off,
and without any sign of lacuna goes on, "For to make precyous
watur for eiȝen þat ben clere and blynde"--what I recognize
as recipe 78 in my standard list (Heinrich, f. 90v). The
scribe has jumped from one text to another in the middle of a
page. The phenomenon is not unknown elsewhere; with material
of this kind it is much harder than usual to recognize, as
the second example may show. On page 262 the rubric "For þe
flux and for þe menysoun" stands as a title just like hundreds
of others in the manuscript; but it is followed immediately by
"Reede cressen ys hoot and drie in þe iij degre þe seed wyl
endure v wynter it is good for to staunche þe flux & for þe
menesoun"--a verbatim extract from *The Virtues of Herbs*. The
original herbal has, as it were, been disguised as a collection
of recipes. The recipe "For to auoide lechery" given as Dawson
577, also found in Add. 4698, f. 53, is of the same nature, in
origin an extract from the "nettle" entry in *The Virtues of
Herbs*. The catalogue entry in the most recent volume of the
British Library catalogue, published in the fall of 1977,[11]
records as containing "recipes" the pages that contain this
and other extracts from this herbal. It could be argued, of
course, that each has become a recipe; but the same pages also
contain a urinoscopy (f. 57) and some definitions of mental
states (f. 68 ff.) found elsewhere too. And Dawson's published
Leechbook numbers consecutively everything that comes, recipes,
extracts from herbals, details of regimen, and suitable days
for bloodletting. Unless our indexers are more alert than
these, the collection, the basis of indexing, is going to be
difficult to identify and list, and all the sub-literary
material of potential interest to linguists and social historians is going to escape the sorting-out that our work is
supposed to effect.

     If indexing by collection is possible, with entries not
greatly dissimilar to those for any other text, what are we
to do with the "casuals," the fly-leaf additions we mentioned
earlier, which are often demonstrably the same as those in the
collections? I think the presence of these ought to be recorded,
with only a ten- or twelve-word extract from the incipit.
Beyond a stated number, perhaps six or ten, "casual" recipes
would be treated as a "collection," but the entry itself would
always make clear how they have been treated. Ultimately, at
the first-line-index stage, it might be necessary to relegate

such casual recipes to an appendix, but the size of such an
appendix, freed from the hundreds if not thousands of entries
that would remain among the collections, would be small. And
any future compiler of a *Corpus Medicamentorum* would have
available, in the list of recipe collections and the appendix
of casual recipes, the material for his task.

Finally, when is a Middle English recipe no longer a Middle
English recipe, or how late do we continue to record relevant
material? For verse, the original Brown and Robbins *Index of
Middle English Verse* took a firm stand on 1500, though Robbins
and Cutler took a more liberal line in the *Supplement*. It
would, I suspect, have been of little use to include much of
later date; new material was superseding the old, though I have
found a copy of *Index of Middle English Verse* 4219 in use as
an epitaph as late as 1696,[12] and variants of number 3220.5
from every century but the present one. But for recipes, continuity was assured for well over a century beyond the date of
1500. I started at first to note as "late survivals" recipes
I recognized in manuscripts in sixteenth-century hands. I soon
gave up and confined myself to seventeenth-century ones, regarding all sixteenth-century ones as automatically to be
treated as relevant. The five specimens I include in the Appendix show, naturally, the same sort of variety as we have already seen (I, for instance, is shortened by haplography (other
versions have "do þerto"), some of which may well be caused
by modernization of vocabulary. They could be paralleled many
times over: even the charms which seem to attract so much of
the attention of those who write about Middle English recipes,
and which are often omitted from late copies, are found in
Ashmole 1453, pp. 160 ff., which contains several dates indi-
cating it was written in 1628 and 1629. But with the exception
of Harley 1734, the medicine book of John Forbes of Echt, which
contains a collection identical with that in Egerton 833, all
the seventeenth-century survivals are of recipes treated individually; the Middle English collection as such is no longer
recognizable.

Whether this change in the status of collections affects
the choice we make for it or not, some clear cut-off date
for recording material I suppose we shall have to have. As we
work to such a date I hope we shall always bear in mind that
in its arbitrariness it is no different from many of the other
working rules under which we operate. An index is, after all,
only a pointer to, and a way of introducing some order into,
the mass of heterogeneous material produced by living men recording, copying, editing, and seeking to pass on the knowledge
of their time.

Henry Hargreaves
University of Aberdeen

NOTES

1. National Library of Wales, Peniarth 403, pp. 239, 241.

2. Peniarth 369, p. 203.

3. Peniarth 394, pp. 49-90, and B.L. Sloane 1201 are specimens.

4. "There is probably a great deal of repetition in this book, besides what has been noted here." *A Catalogue of the Medieval Manuscripts in the University Library, Aberdeen* (Cambridge, 1932), p. 116.

5. *Speculum*, 45 (1970), 393-415.

6. This refers to the cyclostyled "Guide for the Preparation of Index Entries" circulated in advance of the Cambridge Conference, the most important provisions of which were unchallenged during the proceedings.

7. The *"Liber de Diversis Medicinis,"* EETS, o.s. 207 (London, 1938), p. 100.

8. "Medical Manuscripts in Middle English," p. 403.

9. *The Cyrurgie of Guy de Chauliac*, ed. Margaret S. Ogden, EETS, o.s. 265 (London, 1971); examples are on pp. 418-19.

10. Wherever possible, the text has been taken from one of the collections already published. These are: Fritz Heinrich, *Ein mittelenglisches Medizinbuch* (Halle, 1896); G. Henslow, *Medical Works of the Fourteenth Century* (London, 1899); Warren R. Dawson, *A Leechbook* or *Collection of Medical Recipes of the Fifteenth Century* (London, 1934); Margaret S. Ogden, *The "Liber de Diversis Medicinis."* Words in brackets represent my corrections of Dawson.

11. *Catalogue of Additions to the Manuscripts 1756-1782* (London, 1977), p. 186.

12. "Middle English Lyrics in an AUL manuscript," *Aberdeen University Review*, 43 (1969), 153.

APPENDIX

Forty Variants

1. Take peletur of spayne and chewe þe rote þre dayes a good
   quantite and hit shal purge þe heued & do awey þe ache and
   festyn þe teeþ in þe gomes.
                                    Heinrich: Add. 33996, f. 80v

2. Take peletre of spayne and chewe þe rote a good quantyte
   iij dayes and it schal purge þe heed and do away þe ache
   and fastyne þy teeþ in þy gomes
                              Aberdeen U:L: 258, p. 207

3. Take peletyr of spayne and chewe the rote thre dayes a a
   good quantyte and hit schal purge the hed and do awey the
   ache and make fast the teth yn the gommes.
                                    Sloane 963, f. 40

4. Take peletre of spayne and chewe þe rote þre dayes a gode
   quantyte and hit schal purge þe heued and do away ache
   and fasten þe gomes in þe heued wiþ þe tethe.
                                    Paniarth 388, f. 19

5. Take pellettre of spayne & chew the rote iij dayes a good
   quantite & it shal purge the hed & do away the ache of
   the gomes & fasten thy teith in the gomys.
                                    Cosin V.iii.10, f. 27

6. Take pellettre of spayne & chewe the rote a good quantyte
   iij dayes & this shal purge the hed & do way the tothe ache
   & ache of the hed & fasten thy teyth in the gommes.
                                    Cosin, V.iii.10, f. 40

7. Take þe licor of spayn & chew þe roote iij days a good
   quantite & hit shall purge þe hed & do awey þe ache &
   festyn þe tethe.
                                    Sloane 393, f. 159

8. Take pellitorie of spayne and chawe the roote thre dayes a
   good quantite therof and yt wyll do awaye the ach and fasten
   the teethe in the gommes.
                                    Sloane 1072, f. 8 [late xvi]

9. Take peletre of spayne & chewe wel a good quantite of þe
    rote þerof iij dayes and it wele purge wel þe heued and
    make þe teth to stonde faste and þis is proved.

    Sloane 706, f. 148

10. Take peletre of spayne and chewe þe rote iij days and hit
    schal clense þe heed and do away þi warke and fastyne þi
    teeþ.   Aberdeen U:L: 258, p. 167

11. Take pillitory of spaine and vse to chewe the rootes
    therof in your mouth thre dayes together it shall clense
    the heade do away ach and fasten the teethe.

    Sloane 553, f. 5 [early xvii]

12. Take pelletrey of spaine and chew the roote a good quantity
    of it shall doe away the payne and fasten the teeth in
    the gumms.   Sloane 3526, f. 51 [late xvii]

13. Take the rote of perety of spayne and chew hit well a gud
    quantyty & hit shall sporge þe hede do awey the ache &
    faste thy teth in thy gummys.

    Sloane 140, f. 15

14. Take þe rottys off peletre off spayne & schewe yt well in
    þi mowth and vse þis iij dayes and yt schall spurge thyn
    hede and do away the akyng and fastyng þi teeth yn þe gowmes.

    Ashmole 1432, p. 127

15. Chew þe rote of peletre of spayn iij dayes a good quantite
    it purgith & doth away ache & fasteth the goomes in þe
    hede with þe teeth.
    Sloane 405, f. 126v

16. Tak þe rote of peletre of spayne and chewe hit wel bytwen
    þy teþ & hit shal clense þyn heed & don awey þe werkyng &
    fastene þy teþ.   Sloane 540A, f. 10

17. Take the roote of pellitorie of spaine and chafe it betwixt
    the teeth to and fro a good while and it will spurge the
    heade and fasten the teeth.

    Sloane 1017, f. 25v [xvi]

18. Take and chewe pyllatory of spayne iij dayes a good
    quantyte and it wyll purge the heed well and put awaye
    the ache and fasten the tethe.

    Sloane 694, f. 50v [xvi]

19. Tak pilletere & chew þe rote þre dayes & hit schal spurge
     þe heued & benyme þe ach & fasten þe teeþe.

                             Wellcome 406, f. 6v

20. Take peletes and chewe the rott iij daes and hit schal
     sporge thy heed and voiden the ache abd wyll fastyng thy
     teth wel.
                             Wellcome 404, f. 6v

21. Take peletre & chew þe rote iij dayys & it shall clense
     thy hed & do away þe ache & fastyn þy teyth.

                             Sloane 3542, f. 48

22. Take peletus & chewe þe rote iij dayes & hit schal clense
     þy hed & do awey akyng & fastene þy tethe.

                             Royal 12.G.iv, f. 188v

23. Take peletre & chewe þe rote þre dayys & yt shal spurge
     þin heued & fasteny þy teþe.

                             Ashmole 1434, p. 258

24. Take peletre & seþe þe rotes iij dayes & it sal clense
     þin hed & do away þe akyng.

                             Royal 18.A.vi, f. 1

25. Tak peletur & chew it þe rote þerof iij dayes and it sal
     spurge þin hede bynymen þe werke & festyn þi teth.

                             Ashmole 1438 I, p. 6

26. Take pelletre & chew þe rote þeroffe iij daies & it chal
     spurge þin heed benyme þo ake & festen þi teþ.

                             Sloane 962, f. 12

27. R pelletre & chew þe rote þerof þre daies & it schal
     spurge þyn hed & beneme þe ache & [fest]ne þi teþ.

                             Peniarth 370, f. 13

28. Nym peletre & chewe þe rote þerof iij dayes.... spurge
     þyn hed & byneme þe ache & fasten....

                             Bodl. e Mus. 146, f. ii
                             (very badly rubbed)

29. Nym peletre and clarie the rote and vse this thre daies
     and it schal clanse the hed and bynyme the ache of the hed
     and al the greuaunce.   Sloane 2457, f. 10

30. Take peletere rootes and chewe þerof oftesydes iij dayes
    and it schall clense þe heed & beneme þe akynge.

    Sloane 1764, f. 7

31. Take pelleter rotys and chewe hem thre dayes & hit schall
    clense thy hede & do awey aking and festeryng of tethe.

    Sloane 372, f. 21

32. Take þe rote of pelestre & chew it thre daies & it sall
    spurge þe heued & fordo þe wark & festen þhe tethe.

    Arundel 276, f. 9

33. Tak þe rote of peletir & chew it iij dayes & it wille
    purge þe heyd & fordo þe werke and fest þe tethe.

    Sloane 213, f. 138v

34. Take peletre & chew the rote thre dayes & yt schall purge
    thyne hede and festyn thyne tethe.

    Sloane 382, f. 38v

35. Ta pelytre rotys & gnaw þerof iij dayys or iiij & hyt
    shall clanse þe hede.
    Sloane 120, f. 88

36. Chewe a good quantite of peletur of spayne by iij daies &
    it shal pourge the heed.
    Wellcome 408, f. 52

37. Take peletre & chewe it in þi mowthe iij dayes & be hool.

    Hunterian 328, 62v

38. Take peletre and chew þe rothe iij days and be hole.

    Dawson: Med. Soc. London 136,
    f. 1

39. Take þe rote of peleter and chewe hit thre dayes.

    Sloane 372, f. 15

40. Take lynseed and letuse and stampe hem togedur and pelletre
    of spayne and chewe þe roote iij dayes a good quantyte
    and it schal purge þe heed and don away þe ache and fastene
    þe teeþ in þe gomes.

    Aberdeen U.L. 258, p. 275

Twenty-Five Recipes for Head-Ache

A   Take and seþe verueyne and betoyne and wermod and þerwyþ
wasche þe seke heued & þanne make a plasture aboue on þe
moolde on þis manere   Take þe same erbys when þey beon
sodyn and wrynge hem and grynde hem smale in a morter and
tempre hem wyþ þe same licour aʒeyne & do þerto wheton
branne to holde in þe licour and make a garlande of a
kerchef and bynde þe seke heued and ley þe plasture on þe
molde wyþynne þe garlaunde as hoot as þe seke may suffre
and bynde þe hed wyþ a volyper and sette a kappe aboue and
þys do bote þre dayes and þe seke shal be hool on warantyse
(32)

Heinrich: Add. 33996, f. 80v

B   Take peletur of spayne and chewe þe rote þre dayes a good
quantite and hit shal purge þe heued & do away þe ache
and festyn þe teeþ in þe gomes.
(71)

Heinrich: Add. 33996, f. 80v

C   Take þe jus of walwort and salt & hony & wax & encense and
buyle hem togedur ouer þe fuyre and þerwyþ anoynte þe heued
and þe temples
(45)

Heinrich: Add. 33996, f. 81

D1   Take veruayne or vetoyn or filles of wormod and make lee
þerof and wasche þe heued þerwith thrys in a weke
(16)

Ogden: Lincoln Cath. A.5.a,
f. 280

D2   Make þerfor lye of verveyne or ellys of betenye ether of
wormod and þerwith wasshe thyne hede thrise in þe weke
(21)

Dawson: Med. Soc. London 136,
f. 1

D3   Take and make lye of werueyne other of betayne other of
wormwode & therwyth wasche þe hede iij in the weke
(5)

Sloane 382, f. 37v

E   Take wormod wex and encens and stamp heme togeder wyþ the
whyte of an ay and do it in a lynen clout and bynd about
[þin] hede
(17)

[ym] Dawson: Med. Soc. London
136, f. 1

F   Take savayn and stamp hitt and tempyr itt wyþ oyll of rosen
     and seth and anoynt thyne hede þerwyþ agayns the sunne in
     somer and agayns þe fyre in wynter   Do so oft and be hole
     (15)

                              Dawson: Med. Soc. London 136,
                                f. 1

G   Take mustard seed and [ruwe] and stamp hem wele togeder
     and tempre hitt wele wyþ water so þat itt be thykk and lay
     itt to [þin] hede
     (14)

                              [rubb] [ym] Dawson: Med. Soc.
                                London 136, f. 1

H   Take bitayne verveyn celidony wormod weybred [ruwe] walwort
     sawge fyue cornes of peper and hony and seith all in water
     and drynke hitt fastynge
     (29)

                              [rubb] Dawson: Med. Soc. London
                                136, f. 1

I   Take þe gal of an hare & medil it wiþ hony ana & anoynt
     þerwiþ þe hede & þe temples
     (2)

                              Sloane 405, f. 126v.

J   Hete hilwort & eysell and do it in your nose threllys þat
     þe odour may go to þe brayne and make a playster of hilworth
     sodyn and layy itt to your hede
     (6)

                              Dawson: Med. Soc. London 136,
                                f. 1

K   Take an handfull of ruwe and an oþer off hayhove þe þrid
     of leuys of lorec and seith heme togeder in water ether in
     wyne and þat playster lay on [þin] hede and þis is for ach
     þat durith longe
     (3)

                              [ym] Dawson: Med. Soc. London
                                136, f. 1

L   Take *sothernwode and hony & eysell pound it togedir &
     drynk if oft fastyng
     (5)

                              v.l. aueroyne Dawson: Med.
                                Soc. London 136, f. 1

M   Take ruw wyþ the thykke grounde of eufras & enoynt thy
     temples
     (2)
                              Dawson: Med. Soc. London 136,
                                 f. 1v

N   Take puliole & sethe it in vynacre & drynke it & halde thi
     heued ouer þe substance & after emplaster it on thi heuede
     all þe nyghte
     (2)
                              Ogden: Lincoln Cath. A.5.2,
                                 f. 280

O   Take puliole with þe jeuse of þe flour & braye it in a
     mortere & drynke it fastande with hate water & ete noghte
     or none
     (3)
                              Ogden: Lincoln Cath. A.5.2,
                                 f. 280

P   Take encenes & coluere dunge and whete floure an vnce of
     ich and temper hem wyþ þe white of an ey and wherso þe hede
     akyth bynd it and it shall voyd away anone
     (2)
                              Dawson: Med. Soc. London 136,
                                 f. 1v

Q   Take puliol reall & braye it with hony & emplaster it to
     þi hede
     (2)
                              Ogden: Lincoln Cath. A.5.2,
                                 f. 280v

R   Stamp rwe wiþ salt & hony & ley it as a plastere to þe hed
     & þat chal mykel help þe
     (2)
                              Sloane 962, f. 12v

S   Take fenel & rewe and seþe hem wel in watur and wasshe
     þe seek heued and make þerof a plastre in þe maner as hit
     is forsayde
     (10)
                              Heinrich: Add. 33996, f. 86

T   Take of rewe verueyne beteyne wermot sauge walwort heyhoue
     red fenel weybrode ellerne barke ana m   l wasshe clene
     þe erbes and pile þe barke þe ottemoste awey and stampe hem

smale in a morter and nyne bayes and put hem into an erþen
pot and do þerto a potel of good red wyn & anoþer of stale
ale and let hem seþe tille þe haluendel be wasted & at þe
begynnynge put in a quarter of an [vnce] of poudre of pepur
and let hit seþe wyþ þe erbes and take hit doune & streyne
hit & let þe seek drinke þerof ferste and last seuene spon-
fulle at ones at euen hot an morew colde nyne dayes & let þe
seek wasshe his heued wyþ þis licour þat comes aftur and make
a plastur of þeose erbes þat y nemene here aftur. Take rewe
houe betoyne verueyne myntes hilwort red fenel wermot
sowþernewode ana m. l wasche hem clene & schrede hem &
seþe hem in an erþen pot in faire water and wasche þe seke
heued in þat licour & let schaue þe moolde and make a
garlond of ackerchef and make a plastre of þe erbes and þe
lycour & of wheten bren & as hot as þe seek may suffre ley
þe plasture on þe molde & he shal be hool wyþ ynne fyue
plastres at þe ferrest on warantyse bote loke þat þe plastre
be not renued bote ones on þe nyзt and on þe day & bynde a
voluper aboue and a cappe aboue þat and þanne shal nomon
be þe wyser þat þe plasture is aboue
(13)
                         Heinrich: Add. 33996, f. 88

U   Take ache & cherwile and seth it long in watre & soupe
    þerof offte & hold þerof in þi mowth & it sall drawe þe
    warke out at þi mouth or at yne or at þine heres or at
    yneyne
    (6)   Ashmole 1438, p. 7

V   Take þe jeuse of rewe vyneacre & oyle of roses & beres of
    lorell & lay þam to thi heuede   It helpes wonderfully
    (2)
                         Ogden: Lincoln Cath. A.5.2.,
                                   f. 280v

W   Take trefoyl egremonye fenel beteyn aueroyn camamil ana &
    sethe hem in clene water into þe þrid pert   Take þat water
    & wasch þe hede & lay þe herbes to þe temples vnder a voliper
    or a coyffe wel þat þai fal not away

                    Sloane 405, f. 126

Y   Take oile olif & eisil of euyn weyght and styl it agayn þe
    son in a glas & anoynte þe hed.

                    Sloane 405, f. 126

Z   Take walewort and virgyn wax and boyle hem togyder ouer þe
    fyre and anoynte þin hed þerwith
    (3)
                    Henslowe: Harley 2378, p. 237

Some Opening Orders

A-W, Y, Z: as in *"Twenty-Five Recipes"*
X: a "head-ache" recipe not included in twenty-five
?: a "head-ache" recipe, which one not known
x: another recipe, not for a head-ache
*: recipes preceded by title
**: recipes preceded by IMEV 3422 The man þat wole ...

ABC   Aberdeen U.L. 258, p. 207; **Camb. Trinity O.1.13, f. 45v;
C.U.L. Dd.6.29, f. 34; **Arundel 272, f. 1; **Lansdowne
680, f. 21v; **Sloane 382, f. 211; **Sloane 468, f. 7;
Sloane 521, f. 204; Sloane 963, f. 40; Royal Coll.
Physicians 411, f. 1; Wellcome 409, f. 16.

xABC **Camb. Trinity O.1.13, f. 160; Add. 33996, f. 80;
**Harley 1600, f. 3v; Sloane 100, f. 1; **Sloane 374,
f. 14; **Wellcome 542, f. 1; Ashmole 1477 II, f. 1.
[In every case "x" is the recipe "For sausefleme"
printed by Heinrich.]

AST   Aberdeen U.L. 258, p. 273; NLW 572, f. 7; Yale U.L. 163,
f. 82v.

AWY   Sloane 405, f. 126.

xBAC Peniarth 388, f. 19 ["x" is 'For Sausefleme'].

BHG   Sloane 706, f. 107; Sloane 1764, f. 7.

D1EF Lincoln Cath. A.5.2., f. 280; *Sloane 213, f. 138; York
Minster XVI.E.32, f. 14; Arundel 276, f. 9.

D1FG Sloane 3542, f. 48.

D1HV Sloane 372, f. 15.

D2BC *Aberdeen U.L. 258, p. 167.

D2BH *Cosin V.iii.11, f. 30; *Royal 12,G,iv, f. 188v; *Sloane
372, f. 21; *Sloane 521, f. 232; *Sloane 4698, f. 91v;
*Bodley 483, f. 3v.

D2B? *Royal 18.A.vi, f. 1.

D2EF *C.C.C. 388, f. 36v; Sloane 1964, f. 42r; Sloane 2527,
f. 161; *Med. Soc. London 136, f. 1; Ashmole 1432, p. 258.

D2Ex *Sloane 610, f. 6v.

D2FG Peniarth 370, f. 13; Bodl. e Mus. 146, f. ii.

D2HB *Sloane 2581, f. 5 [elaborated title].

D2HZ Harley 2378, p. 237.

D3EF   Hunterian 328, f. 62v; *Sloane 382, f. 37v.

D3FG   *Sloane 964, f. 2; Sloane 964, f. 43.

GBU   Sloane 962, f. 12; Ashmole 1438, p. 6.

JD2x   Camb. St John's 37.II, f. 11.

T1BF   *Sloane 540A, f. 9v.

T1Bx   *Sloane 393, f. 22v; *Royal 17.A.xxxii, f. 43.

xxx   C.U.L. Ee.1.13, f. 101; Cosin V.iv.1, f. 23; Cosin
        V.iii.10, f. 24; Add. 34111; Sloane 96, f. 1; Sloane
        374, f. 61; Sloane 3217, f. 79; Ashmole 1438, p. 83.

Specimen Seventeenth-Century Copies

I   Take pyliall royall piliall mounteyn baynwort ambrose
ribwort bugle celydoyne therfoyle weybrede morell tansey
betayn of each elich moch and stamp heme wele togedir with
swynes grese fresshe & frankyn encens a lyttyll hony and
virgyne wax and when all thies things bene wele stamped
togedir do hem in a clene basyne or a panne & þerto white
wyne and let it stand all a day and all a nyȝt & on the
morrow do it to the fire & seth it wele and gif it good
walme afterwarde do it down and draw it thorow a cloth &
do it up & the while it is ought sore enoynt it þerwith
and it shall hele hyme full wele.

> Dawson: Med. Soc. London 136,
> f. 8v

Tak pullioll riall pullioll muntane branwort ambriss
ribebugle seterak celdon charuefull reid nettell leikis
ache wabraid morellis tansay wetoyn of ilkane alyk mekill
and stamp þam samen with swynes creiss & lelle honny &
wirginne wax and quhan all thir thingis ar weill stampit
than yow do thaim in ane clene bassine or in ane panne
and do it up (sic) and it þat is sair anoynt þairwith and
it sall help him weill.

> Harley 1734, f. 6v. Written
> by Patrick Scott for the
> "Medicine Book" of John Forbes
> of Echt, Aberdeenshire, 1605.

II   *Ad clarificandum oculos destruendum perlam & le hawe in
oculo generata*   Take red rooses, smalache, rewe, verueyne
maydenher eufrace endyue sengrene hilwort reed fenel
celydoyne ana quarter [pound] wasshe hem clene and ley
hem in good whit wyn a day and a nyȝt after stille hem in
a stillatorye and þe ferste water wol be like to gold þe
secounde as seluer þe þridde as baume and kepe þat in a
viol of glas for hit is worþe baume for any maner of
malady of þe sore yen

> Heinrich: Add. 33996, f. 91

*A precious water to claryfye the yes and to do awaye the
pearle or webbe*   Take redrose smalage rewe verveyne
maydenhere comfrie emore sengrene hillworte redfenell
celedeyne ana iiij oz and wasshe them cleane & laye them
in whighte wyne a daye and a nyght. Then still yt in a
stillytory the ffirste water ys like goulde the secounde

ₗike silver and the thirde like balme and kepe this in a
glasse for yt ys worthie baume for many and divers
maladyes and sore yene.
Sloane 1000, f. 94v: A large
collection of recipes, apparently collected by M. Gedeon
Bonnivert; many are dated, all
within the seventeenth century
and the latest on the back of
a printed document dated 1693
(f. 232). The collection from
f. 90 to f. 97 seems somewhat
older than that.

*A pretious water to destroy a pearle in a mans eye sight
and to cleare the eyes* Take redrose campion red fennell
rew vervine eufras endive betony of each alike so that you
have 6 handfulls of them all steepe them all in a pottle
of white wine a day and a night distill them in a stillotory
and the first water that shall be like gold the second like
siluer and the third like balme vse to drop 2 or 3 drops
of this water evening and morning it will destroy the
pearle this water is also pretious for gentlewomen in
steede of balme.
Sloane 3526, f. 53v in a late
seventeenth-century hand; one
of several recipes (including
one in the "Forty Variants")
there described as "written
in the old Countesse of
Arundells boke."

III   *Contra apostema vel passiones inueteratas .i. le stiche*
Take þe rote of þe holy hocke & wasche hyt clene & seeþ
hyt tyl hyt be tender & þan poure out þe water in to a
vessel & take lynsed & fenngreke ana but loke þou haue of
hem to as meche as of þe rote when hyt ys ysoden by wyȝt
& let seþe þe lynsed & þe fenngreke in þe same water þat
þe hocke was soden inne ryȝt wel tyl hyt be ropynge as
bryd lym & þat þe same lycour be welnye ysoden awey & þe[n]
stampe þe rote & do hyt þerto & put þerto barly mele &
medele hem wel togedre & frye hem vp wyþ barowes grece
& ley þe plastre to þe sore as hote as þe seke may suffree
hyt & vse þys medycne for wyþ þynne nye plastres he schal
be hole.
Heinrich: Add. 33996, f. 105

Middle English Recipes 11.

*To destroye an Impostume or stitche in whate place soever
it be* Take the roote of hollihock wash it cleane & seethe
it till it be tender then power oute the water into a
vessell and take lyneseede and ffenygreke of either alike
moche but look that you haue as moche of them two as of
the roote when it is soden by waight and seethe the
lynseede and the venygreke in the same water that the
hollihock roote was sodden in vntill it be roppinge as
birdlyme And when the same liquore is wellnigh sodden
away then stampe the roote and put it therto and put
therto barly meale myngle them well together and frye them
with barrowes grease and make a plaster therof and apply
it as hoate as may be suffered and vse this plaster nine
tymes and you shalbe whole.

> Sloane 553, f. 58. Owners'
> dates of 1635 and 1639 are
> given, and the handwriting
> is of the same period.

For to destroy all Impostumes either in man or woman
Take þe roote of hollihocke and wash it cleane and seeth
it till it be tender and then put the water into a vessell
and then take linseed and fenegreke of each of them a like
much and see þat you haue as much of them two as þe roote
þat is sodden Then seeth them in þe same water till it
rope as it were Birdlime then stamp þe roote and do thereto
Barly meale and mingle them well together and fry them
with Boris greace and lay it to þe sore plaisterwise as
hot as you may suffer it and within nyne days yee shalbee
whole.

> Sloane 712, f. 6, one of three
> sections (with Sloane 1121
> and Sloane 792) of a collection
> of recipes in a seventeenth-
> century hand.

THE MANUSCRIPTS OF NICHOLAS LOVE'S
MYRROUR OF THE BLESSED LYF OF JESU CHRIST
AND RELATED TEXTS

The choice of Love's *Myrrour* and other anonymous English versions of the *Meditationes Vitae Christi* as suitable texts to discuss at a conference on Middle English prose needs little justification. Margaret Deanesley's statement, made in 1920, "Love's *Myrrour* ... had an interesting history, and was probably more popular than any other single book in the fifteenth century ..." (*Modern Language Review*, 15 [1920], 353) has been substantially reaffirmed and extended by more recent research upon the *Myrrour* and related treatises.[1] Its popularity has been established beyond doubt by the almost continuous discovery of surviving manuscripts: since 1908, when L.F. Powell produced his edition of the work, and cited twenty-three manuscripts, twenty-four more have emerged, and there is no reason to suppose that the supply is exhausted. In addition to the forty-nine complete manuscript copies listed below, there are a number of fragments of complete manuscripts, as well as evidence of its circulation as a Passion narrative only. With regard to the anonymous--and partial--English versions of the *Meditationes*, many manuscripts are known to us, representing nine different treatments of the Latin; other large-scale *Lives of Christ and the Virgin* make serious use of the *Meditationes*. In addition to this numerical filling-in of the picture of manuscript production, much more is still coming to light about the conditions in which the copies of these vernacular treatises were produced. The identification of scribes, the identification of the language of the manuscripts, and the clarification of the general context of patronage and ownership are all areas of current research activity in England and in the United States. So also is the inquiry into the literary relationships of the *Myrrour* with other anonymous Lives of Christ and Passion treatises--both those which make a strict use of the *Meditationes*, and those which are also indebted more freely to a wide area of Latin devotional prose.

We must ask, however, what relevance such materials and processes have to the particular occasion of the Conference--

the marking of the inauguration of the *Index of Middle English Prose*. Much has already been said, in formal and informal session, of the need to simplify the necessarily laborious tasks of the contributors to the first stage of the *Index*-- the Handlists of prose items in medieval manuscripts. But there is, in my view, much more to be said about the essential "two-way relationship" between the work which will be required in order to present the *Index* in its second and final form, and that work which is already involved in the research I have described. Each must be, to a significant and increasing extent, dependent upon the other in order to function properly. Ideally, the structure brought into being by the production and completion of the *Index* should not only be able to provide an accurate and, indeed, definitive account of texts and their manuscripts; it should also, by reason of its very existence, be prepared to act as a cohesive and coordinating force upon the very various kinds of pursuit which engage us when we use the *Myrrour* or any other wealthily-connected work as a guide to the larger landscapes of Middle English religious prose, and see its history as a map of literary, devotional, bibliographical, and dialectal factors. If we can take a liberal as well as a realistic view of our responsibilities, we should be able to make sure that important information about a text and its affiliations which may be discovered in the course of work by *Index* contributors, as well as in the course of other species of research, is codified properly and absorbed into scholarly consideration. I think here, particularly, of the application to the *Myrrour* and connected translations of that intensive (and comprehensive) study of medieval scribal activity in England which is at present proceeding from centers in Oxford, Cambridge, Durham, and Edinburgh, and is associated with Professor Angus McIntosh, Dr. A.I. Doyle, Dr. Malcolm Parkes, Mr. Jeremy Griffiths, and Dr. Richard Beadle. I think also of the relevance of descriptive analysis of fifteenth-century book decoration and workshop allegiance, by art historians such as Dr. Jonathan Alexander and Dr. Kathleen Scott. And I think of my own interest in the collection and ordering of data on book-patronage and ownership among fifteenth-century nobility and gentry.[2] Those who move in multiple fields of research know how important it is to be made cognizant not only of studies but also of specialist skills which may be unexpectedly rewarding; the purposes of *Index* contributors and scholars and critics in related fields may have to be collaborative, as the task of recognition and definition of manuscript items draws upon knowledge to be gained only through research experience, and the pleasure of creative interpretation is sustained by precise information about materials to be gained only through patient inquiry and record.

This "inter-connectedness" can be illustrated even from a
speculative forecast of the problems to be encountered in what
might appear to be the comparatively straightforward business
of listing the manuscripts of Love's *Myrrour* for the final
Index entry. The choice, for instance, of the most authoritative text as head-entry will involve judgments of the most
varied nature and will return the *Index* contributor to the
historical situation for which the *Myrrour* was produced--a
situation well described by Dr. A.I. Doyle when commenting
upon the agreement among its manuscripts as to form and quality,
and upon the very slight textual variation which they display:

> it is probable that these characteristics originate in
> the care and precision with which the author disposed
> his composition and its publication ... and were main-
> tained by the simplicity of the text and its reproduc-
> tion by experienced hands.[3]

Nevertheless, the necessity of choice laid upon the *Index*
contributor will also necessitate a more rigorous examination
of the nature of that "slight textual variation"--if not to be
undertaken by the contributor, then by others whose advice may
be sought. It will probably be desirable to keep in mind the
special circumstances in which the *Myrrour* was completed--at
Mount Grace, in Yorkshire, then brought down to London for approbation by Arundel of Canterbury and for publication as a
weapon of orthodoxy to combat Lollard doctrine. In this context, the "authority" of early manuscript copies of northern
provenance and language--C.U.L. Add. 6578, for instance--will
be significantly tested against those of metropolitan origin
and character.

But apart from the minutiae of the internal relationships
of the *Myrrour* manuscripts, there is the question of the relationship of the *Myrrour* to other vernacular versions of the
Meditationes. It might, indeed, be thought that this is of
little concern to the *Index*, even in its ultimate format; we
can, however, demonstrate that if the information provided by
the *Index* is not only to record the existence of prose texts,
but also, finally, to identify them as far as possible, attention will have to be paid to the frequently hybrid nature of
these medieval English narratives of the Life of Christ and the
Virgin. Here again the *Index* contributor must, to some extent,
be guided by the researcher, or engage himself in that kind of
close inspection of materials which is an essential part of
research procedure. An account of manuscripts of the *Myrrour*
cannot be complete without taking note of the possibility that
Love's translation may appear as a section in a quite different,
composite prose work; nor can we be confident about our ability

to enumerate and characterize the various anonymous renderings
of the *Meditationes* if we do not envisage that our research
into them may take us back to the manuscripts of the *Myrrour*
itself.
    Camb. Trinity B.2.18, at present catalogued simply as a
"Life of Christ and the Virgin," contains, in fact, three
separate "units" of material: a prefatory narrative of the Fall
and Flood; an anonymous translation of the *Meditationes* up to
the Die Jovis chapter; Love's own translation of the Latin text
from that point onwards. The Foyle and Takamiya 20 manuscripts
of the *Myrrour* incorporate, unexpectedly, and in uncommented
sequence, a partial translation of the Die Veneris chapter of
the *Meditationes*, known from at least six other manuscript
copies. (See below, Appendix, section 2(A)(ii).) The problems
presented by the three manuscripts are both technical and more
widely contextual, but it is doubtful whether on either score
they can be quite irrelevant to the making of the appropriate
Index entries in their final form. From a technical point of
view, the problem facing the *Index* contributor is how to record
the phenomena displayed: the third section of B.2.18 must be
listed among other "partial" copies of Love's *Myrrour*; the
second section must be recorded as an independent, if partial,
translation of the *Meditationes*, and the intrusive Passion narrative of the Foyle and Takamiya 20 manuscripts must be listed
among other copies of a terse, southern rendering of the *Meditationes*. Attention to nothing but the introductory or framing
matter of the manuscript items involved could give an entirely
false set of leads to those who may turn to consult the *Index*.
The wider problems referred to above concern the interpretation
of the phenomena displayed by the manuscripts. What reason did
the "author" or scribe of B.2.18 have for using only part of
Love's translation? Was that translation circulated first of
all as a version of the central Die Jovis and Die Veneris chapters of the *Meditationes*? Indications that this might have been
so are given by such manuscripts as Bodley Eng. th. c.58 which
contains a Passion narrative only of the *Myrrour*.[4] (See below,
Appendix, Section 1(B).) What reason did the scribes of the
Foyle and Takamiya 20 manuscripts have for copying out two
parallel translations of the Die Veneris chapter of the *Meditationes*? What do these "editorial processes," so apparently
enigmatic, tell us of the relationship of Love's translation to
earlier, and anonymous, versions of the Latin text?[5] These are
questions which bear interestingly upon matters of authorship
and the possible reintegration of fragmented works; they also
bear upon the possibility of rewriting, in a particularly effective way, that mixed history of the shaping of Latin medita-
tive materials for vernacular and didactic purposes which supports and surrounds Nicholas Love's major contribution: the

Myrrour of the Blessed Lyf of Jesu Christ. It is for these
reasons, above all, that the *Index* will ignore, at peril to
its usefulness, the complex and largely unexplored connections
not only between those texts and manuscripts under discussion,
but also between them and many other English Lives of Christ
and Passion treaties, based, however indirectly, upon the
Meditationes and a variety of affective sources (see below,
Appendix, sections 2 and 3).

Even minor literary curiosities concealed within such narratives may be of importance to the *Index* contributor. Michigan
State College 1 (formerly Phillips 1054), an independent rendering of the Die Veneris section of the *Meditationes*, moves,
for the speech of the Virgin over the dead Christ, into an
elaborately rhythmical and alliterative mode of composition.[6]
It is not clear whether this is in fact a separate "encapsula-
ted" piece, with different originals from the rest of the text;
neither is it clear whether its literary form is prose or unrhymed verse. The relationship here to be investigated is with
Passion narrations in the person of the Virgin, of which there
are a considerable number, Latin and vernacular, verse and
heightened prose. (See below, Appendix, section 3(A).) It is
a relationship, however, which could well be as crucial to the
formulation of an accurate *Index* entry as it may be to the
writing of devotional and literary history.

Last, we might hope that among the data given by the *Index*
entries in their finished state, researchers will find a
variety of signals relevant to their special needs. It would,
for instance, be immensely helpful if medieval punctuation
could be retained in the quotation of opening words from the
texts; it would be even more helpful if some indication could
be given of whether the punctuation in use throughout the texts
is fairly full and consistent, repaying, therefore, further
study. In the case of the manuscripts of the *Myrrour*, it has
already been possible to characterize one finely coherent system of punctuation in a copy historically connected with the
Charterhouse of Mount Grace, where Love was Prior: C.U.L. Add.
6578.[7] And much more might be discovered, from analyses of
manuscript punctuation, about the nature and location of the
scriptoria in which the numerous manuscripts of the *Myrrour*
were produced.

A simple record, too, of the presence of miniature-work or
border-decoration, and of heraldic devices, would alert the
art historian and the historian of literary culture to materials
for further investigation. The importance of such record is
partly, of course, that it contributes to our knowledge of the
historical settings and functions of particular copies of the
Myrrour and related treatises. Thus, the attention of Dr.
Jonathan Alexander to Advocates' 18.1.7--one of the two copies

of the *Myrrour* with miniatures--has determined that the seven-
teen illustrations were made by an artist of the London workshop of William Abell, on single sheets inserted into the
text;[8] the language of the copy has, however, some distinctly
northern characteristics, and in deciding where it was made,
we should note that the coat of arms, on folio 5v, is that of
Edmund Grey, 4th Baron Grey of Ruthyn, who married Lady
Catherine Percy, daughter of the Earl of Northumberland, some
time after 1450. Even when there is less to work on than this,
the art specialist, faced with the frequently lavish border-
decorations of the Love manuscripts--Trinity B.15.16, for instance, or Takamiya 8--could no doubt substantiate and confirm
our understanding of their "local habitation" by means of
meticulous stylistic analysis. Takamiya 8 was owned by Joan,
Countess of Kent, wife of the original founder of Mount Grace,
and given by her to "Alice Belacyse,"[9] a member of an old Yorkshire family; we should not neglect any available key to its
intriguing history.

Looking at these matters in a wider context, the assembling
of data on ownership and on the workshop characteristics--
whether those of script, punctuation, or decoration--allows us
to see how, on the family trees of the English aristocracy of
the fifteenth century, the manuscripts of Love's *Myrrour* hang,
like modest fruit, beside more splendid products of the illu-
minator's art. If Advocates' 18.1.7 was made for the marriage
of Joan Percy to Edmund Grey, we should also notice the Percy
ownership of *Psalters* as beautiful as the companion piece to
Dyson-Perrins 12.[10] Glasgow University Library Gen. 1130 be-
longed to Robert, Lord Willoughby of Eresby (d. 1452); his
daughter-in-law, Joan, Baroness Willoughby, owned a richly illustrated *Book of Hours* of one "Beaufort Saints Workshop," now
B.L. Add. 27948.[11] Bodl. e Mus. 35, which certainly has the
Beaufort arms on the border of page xvi, has also, as Dr. Doyle
assures me, on that same page the obliterated (but visible
under ultra-violet light) arms of the Nevilles. This, and the
initials M and N in the lower corners of the page, take us
back to the interconnected families of Neville and Beaufort,
whose names are constantly associated, during the earlier fifteenth century, with possession of de luxe volumes from the
fashionable workshops of England and the Continent. Joan
Beaufort, daughter of John of Gaunt by his third marriage,
Countess of Westmorland by her own marriage to Ralph Neville,
was both patroness (of Hoccleve) and book owner.[12] It is an
interesting additional fact that Joan Beaufort's nephew, John
Beaufort, Duke of Somerset, married Margaret Holland, grand-
daughter of Thomas de Holand, founder of Mount Grace.

If the making and finishing of the *Index* persuades us to
subject all the manuscripts under discussion to exhaustive

inspection, and to evaluate, no less than order, the results
of such inquiry, we shall indeed be in its debt; the *Index* may
find, equally, that its own debts to current research will be
both inevitable and considerable.

Elizabeth Salter
University of York

NOTES

1. See E. Salter, *Nicholas Love's "Myrrour of the Blessed
Lyf of Jesu Christ," Analecta Cartusiana*, No. 10 (Salzburg,
1974).

2. See, for instance, A.I. Doyle and M.B. Parkes, "The
Production of Copies of the *Canterbury Tales* and the *Confessio
Amantis* in the Early 15th Century," from *Medieval Scribes,
Manuscripts and Libraries*, ed. M.B. Parkes and A.G. Watson
(London, 1978). And see J. Alexander, "William Abell,
'lymnour,' and 15th Century English Illumination," *Kunsthis-
torische Forschungen: Otto Paecht* (Salzburg, 1972), pp. 166-70;
K.L. Scott, "A Mid-Fifteenth Century English Illuminating Shop
and Its Customers," *Journal of the Warburg and Courtauld In-
stitutes*, 31 (1968), 170-96; E. Salter, Introduction to *Troilus
and Criseyde: A Facsimile Edition of Corpus Christi College,
Cambridge, MS. 61* (Ipswich, 1978).

3. A.I. Doyle, unpublished research; quoted in Salter,
Nicholas Love's "Myrrour," p. 15.

4. In this connection, it is interesting to note the exis-
tence of a Latin recension of the Passion chapters of the
Meditationes--the *Meditationes de Passione Christi*, by some
attributed more firmly to St. Bonaventure than the *Meditationes
Vitae Christi* itself. See the edition of M.J. Stallings
(Washington, D.C., 1965) and a recent discussion of the attribu-
tion by Edmund College, O.S.A., in *Franciscan Studies*, 36,
Annual 14 (1976), 106-107.

5. For a preliminary assessment of this, see E. Zeeman
(Salter), "Continuity and Change in English Versions of the
Meditationes Vitae Christi," Medium Aevum, 26 (1957), 25-31.

6. See E. Salter, "Alliterative Modes and Affiliations in
the 14th Century," *Neophilologische Mitteilungen*, 79 (1978),
25-35.

7. See E. Zeeman (Salter). "Punctuation in an Early MS. of
Love's *Myrrour," Review of English Studies*, n.s. 7 (1956),
11-18.

8. See Alexander, op. cit.

9. See f. 120.

10. Illuminated in the early fourteenth century, and now in the collection of Mr. Clark Stillman, New York. See *Gothic Art in Europe, 1270-1330* (Providence, Rhode Island, 1977), no. 45.

11. For the "Beaufort Saints Workshop," see M. Rickert, "The So-Called Beaufort Hours and York Psalter," *Burlington Magazine*, 104 (1962), 238-46; and J. Watts, "Herman Scheere and the Master of the Beaufort Saints," unpublished research, York, 1973.

12. Thomas Beaufort, Duke of Exeter, left a "Tristram" to his sister, Joan, in 1426; John Beaufort, Duke of Somerset, nephew of Joan Beaufort, who married Margaret Beauchamp, owned the Beauchamp Psalter (B.L. Royal 2.A.xviii); George Neville, Baron Abergavenny, Joan Beaufort's grandson, owned the Neville Hours (Berkeley Castle, private collection); Cecily Neville, Duchess of York, daughter of Joan Beaufort, left her volume of "Bonaventura and Hilton" to her niece in 1495. See Salter, *Nicholas Love's "Myrrour,"* and Introduction to *Troilus and Criseyde*, op. cit. We should probably record here the recent edition of *La Vie de Nostre Dame* edited by M. Meiss and E.H. Beatson (New York, 1977) which, in its Introduction, deals with the distinguished ownership of a comparable French translation of the *Meditationes*, and its illustration by the Colombe workshop of fifteenth-century Paris.

APPENDIX

THE MANUSCRIPTS OF NICHOLAS LOVE'S "MYRROUR OF THE
BLESSED LYF OF JESU CHRIST" AND OF RELATED TEXTS

Prefatory Note: In the compilation of this list I have been
generously assisted by Dr. A.I. Doyle.

1. *Myrrour of the Blessed Lyf*

    (A) *Complete Texts*

        British Library Manuscripts

Royal 18.C.x	Mid-fifteenth century
Arundel 112	Fifteenth century
Arundel 364	Fifteenth century
Add. 11565	Fifteenth century
Add. 19901	Early fifteenth century
Add. 30031	Early fifteenth century
Add. 21006	Early fifteenth century

        Oxford Manuscripts

        (a) The Bodleian Library:

Bodley 131	Mid-fifteenth century, written about 1440, by John Morton of York
Bodley 634	Fifteenth century
Bodley 207	Mid-fifteenth century
Bod. e Mus. 35	Earlier fifteenth century
Rawlinson A. 387B	Fifteenth century
Hatton 31	Later fifteenth century

        (b) The College Libraries:

Wadham College 5	Fifteenth century
University College 123	First half of fifteenth century
Brasenose College e.ix	Written about 1430

        Cambridge Manuscripts

        (a) The University Library:

Hh.I.11	Fifteenth century
Ll.iv.3	Fifteenth century
Mm.v.15	Fifteenth century
Add. 6578	Early fifteenth century
Add. 6686	First half of the fifteenth century

(b) The College Libraries
     and Museums:
     Corpus Christi 142   Mid-fifteenth century
     Corpus Christi 143   Fifteenth century
     Trinity B.15.16   First half of fifteenth
                                   century
     Trinity B.15.32   Fifteenth century
     Fitzwilliam Museum:
       McClean 127   Fifteenth century
       Bradfer-Lawrence 9   Fifteenth century

Manuscripts in Other Collections
     Lambeth Palace 328   Fifteenth century
     National Library of   Second half of fifteenth
       Scotland, Advocates'   century
       18.1.7
     Hunterian Library, Uni-   Third quarter of the
       versity of Glasgow,   fifteenth century
       T.3.15
     University Library,   Mid-fifteenth century
       Glasgow, Gen. 1130
     Chetham's Library,   Early fifteenth century
       Manchester, 6690
     Ryland's Library, Man-
       chester:
       Eng. 94   Fifteenth century
       Eng. 98   Fifteenth century
       Eng. 413   Fifteenth century
     Foyle   Early fifteenth century
     Longleat   Fifteenth century
     Leeds Diocesan Archives   Fifteenth century
     Takamiya 4 (formerly   Mid-fifteenth century
       Phillips 8820)
     Takamiya 8 (formerly   Early fifteenth century
       Saumarez)
     Takamiya 20 (formerly   Mid-fifteenth century
       Gage)
     Yale, Beinecke Library:
       324   c. 1430
       535   Fifteenth to sixteenth
                                   century
     Huntington Library:
       HM 1339   Earlier fifteenth century
       HM 149   Earlier fifteenth century
     Pierpont Morgan Library,
       226   Mid-fifteenth century
       648   First half of fifteenth
                                   century

Princeton University Library, Kane 21	Mid-fifteenth century
Illinois University Library, 65	Fifteenth century

(B) *Extracts from "The Myrrour"*

Bodley Eng. th. C.58 (*Die Veneris* Narrative)	Mid-fifteenth century
C.U.L. Ii.iv.9 (two extracts from *Treatise on the Sacrament*)	Fifteenth century
B.L. Harley 4011 (*Prayer to the Sacrament*)	Fifteenth century

(C) *Fragments of Complete MSS of "The Myrrour"*

Bodley Eng. th. f.10 (part of *Die Dominica* chapter)	First half of fifteenth century
C.U.L. Oo.vii.45(i) (part of *Die Veneris* chapter)	Mid-fifteenth century
East Sussex County Record Office (part of *Die Jovis* chapter)	Fifteenth century
University of Missouri --Columbia, fragment No. 174 (part of *Die Lune* chapter)	Fifteenth century
Worcester Cathedral Library c.1.8	
P.R.O. Exchequer K.R. Misc. Book 1.26: a contents list	
no. 1985 in Ker, N., *Pastedowns in Oxford Bindings*	

(D) *Composite Texts, Incorporating Parts of "The Myrrour" and Other Translations*

Camb. Trinity B.2.18
  (Narrative of Fall and
  Flood, Early Life of
  the Virgin, Life of

Christ, using Love's
translation of the *M.V.C.*
from the raising of Lazarus
onwards)
Takamiya 20 and Foyle
(*Myrrour of the Blessed
Lyf*, incorporating anonymous Passion narrative:
see 2(A)(ii) below)

2. *Independent Translations or Adaptations of the M.V.C.*

(A) *Passion Narratives*

(i) *The "Privity of the Passion"*
Camb. Trinity B.10.12   Northern
Durham University Cosin
  Library, V.iii.8
Lincoln Cathedral Library,
  91
Princeton University
Library

(ii) C.U.L. Ii.iv.9   Southern
Camb. Caius 669
Bodl. Bodley 789
Camb. Trinity B.14.38
Laud Misc. 23
Edingurgh University Library,
  Laing 65
Takamiya 20
Foyle

(iii) B.L. Egerton 2658
Rylands Library, Manchester,
  Eng. 895
Stonyhurst College, B.xliii

(iv) Camb. Magdalene Pepys 2125

(v) Michigan State College 1
  (formerly Phillips 1054)

(vi) Laud Misc. 174
Windsor Chapel E.1.1 (events
  after the death of Christ)

(B) *Lives of Virgin and Christ*

  (i)   Camb. Trinity B.15.42
        Bodley 578

  (ii)   Dublin Trinity 423
        Chetham's Library, Manchester,
          MUN.A.2.166
        (Narrative of Fall and Flood,
          Early Life of the Virgin,
          Life of Christ up to Raising
          of Lazarus: corresponds to
          parts I and II of Camb.
          Trinity B.2.18 (see I(D) above)

  (iii) *The "Short reule of the liif of oure lady"*
          (translation of Chapter III of *M.V.C.*)
        British Library MSS:
          Harley 1022
          Harley 2339
          Royal 8.C.i
        Bodley 938
        Ashmole 41
        Camb. Magdalene Pepys 2125

3. *Related Texts dealing with the Life of Christ*

  (A) *Passion Narratives* (narration by the Virgin)

    (i)   Huntington 144
          Camb. Magdalene Pepys 2498
          Leeds University Library
            Brotherton 501

    (ii)   C.U.L. Ii.4.9
          Longleat 29
          Bodley 596
          B.L. Cotton Cleopatra D.VII

  (B) *Complete Lives: The "Speculum Devotorum"*

          C.U.L. Gg.1.6
          Foyle (Beeleigh Abbey,
           Maldon)

PROBLEMS IN MIDDLE ENGLISH
MYSTICAL PROSE

In his seminal study *Western Mysticism*, Dom Cuthbert Butler remarked that the mystics may be studied in three distinct ways: (1) for their religious philosophy and theology; (2) for material for psychophysiology which investigates such phenomena as auto-suggestion, auto-hypnotism, ecstasy, and trance; and (3) as a religious experience.[1]

This rather restrictive attitude was prevalent during the first part of this century and even beyond, with the Butler adherents holding that only those with these specialized interests and expertise were capable of dealing with mystical texts. Yet to follow this dictum would be to ignore the manuscript traditions, literary value, ongoing contribution to the development of English prose, historical and cultural witness, and importance for the history of ideas which the mystical canon entails.

According to Evelyn Underhill, mystics cannot be cut out of their background and judged by spiritual standards alone: "Every mystic is profoundly influenced by his environment and cannot be understood in isolation to it. He is rooted in the religious past of his race, as well as its religious present."[2] This element of tradition includes "all that spiritual culture which the writer has inherited from the past and hands on to the future, and which gives him the framework, the convention, within which his own direct experience can be related."[3] Fortunately, as a sweep of the scholarship of the past seventy-five years reveals, the major scholars of the English mystics indeed saw and developed the wide spectrum of research potential in the mystical corpus, and helped to provide the impetus for the renascence of the medieval English mystics in our own time. One has only to point to the increasing number of critical editions, translations, and modernizations of the mystic writings, the rise in academic courses and dissertations on the mystics, the appearance within the past four years of three publications concerned solely with mysticism-- the *14th-Century English Mystics Newsletter*, the *Journal of Studies in Mysticism*, published in Australia, and *Studia Mystica*--and most recently,

the Paulist Press's Classics of Western Spirituality, a sixty-
volume series dedicated to bringing the great works of Western
mysticism to the general reading public. Fittingly, the first
volume of the series is Julian of Norwich's *Revelations*. Still
another indication of this renascence is the growth of dialogue,
seeking a synthesis of Eastern and Western mysticism. It may
just be that our own age, like the fourteenth century, is
apocalyptic in its orientation, especially as we approach the
second millennium, and craves the optimism, inner peace, hope,
and sense of human purpose inherent in the mystics' way of
life and writings. Or, echoing the words of Anne Groh Seesholtz, referring to the phenomenon of the *Gottesfreunde*: "Do
chaotic times tend to create God-centered groups ... around
leaders of spiritual insight and of daring thoughts, especially
if they emphasize the dignity of man and the possibility of
his understanding the world in which he lives."[4]

The ever-increasing interest in the works of Richard Rolle,
the *Cloud* author, Julian of Norwich, Walter Hilton, and Margery
Kempe affirms Dom David Knowles' observation that "the English
mystics ... form a group which, for the force and purity of
their traditional doctrine, and for the unusual attractions,
both of their personalities and of their style of writing ...
is unequalled by any other single regional or national group
in the later medieval world."[5] Surely, in the vast body of
Middle English prose writings which the *Index* will assess,
other manuscripts of their works, along with anonymous texts
and translations from Latin or continental vernacular texts,
will come to light. And this possibility touches on my own
special interest in and support of the *Index of Middle English
Prose*.

There are several leading problems concerning Middle English
mystical prose writings, which must be considered at this
stage of the *Index*: (1) agreeing upon a clear definition of
mysticism and what constitutes a mystical work, which, in turn,
will affect (2) the question of an organizational schema for
Middle English religious, devotional, and mystical prose;
(3) the specific difficulties attendant upon Middle English
translations of continental works, both in Latin and the ver-
naculars, and subsequent translations of Middle English works
into Latin; (4) the omnipresent problem of false ascriptions,
acephalous works, multiple titles, compilations, and interpolations; and (5) the continuing transmission of mystical texts
throughout the fifteenth, sixteenth, and seventeenth centuries,
and beyond, within England and abroad, in the wake of the Recusant Movement.

Regarding a definition of mysticism, I turn again to Dom
Butler:

There is probably no more misused word in these our days
than mysticism. It has come to be applied to many things
of many kinds; to theosophy and Christian science; to
spiritualism and clairvoyance; to demonology and witch-
craft; to occultism and magic; to weird psychical ex-
periences, if only they have some religious colour; to
revelations and visions; to otherworldliness, or even
mere dreaminess and impracticality in the affairs of
life; to poetry and painting and music of which the motif
is unobvious and vague; it has been identified with the
attitude of the religious mind that cares not for dogma
or doctrine, for church or sacraments; it has been identified also with a certain outlook on the world--a seeing
God in nature, and recognizing that material creation in
various ways symbolizes spiritual realities; a beautiful
and true concept, and one that was very dear to St.
Francis of Assisi, but which is not mysticism according
to its historical meaning. It has been said that the
love of God is mysticism; or that mysticism is only the
Christian life lived on a high level; or that it is Roman
Catholic piety in extreme form.[6]

Or, to quote Phyllis Hodgson, "Mysticism is a word which starts
in 'mist' and ends in 'schism.'"[7]
  Evelyn Underhill defines mysticism in its historical and
psychological dimensions as "the direct intuition or experience
of God," and a mystic as "a person who has, to a greater or
lesser degree, such a direct experience."

The Christian mystic therefore is one for whom God and
Christ are not merely objects of belief, but living facts
experimentally known at first hand, and mysticism ...
becomes ... a life based on this conscious communion
with God ... a communion which is always one of love.[8]

Father William Johnston, among others, points out that "medie-
vals identified mystical theology with mystical experience,
and called contemplation mystical theology,"[9] iterating the
definition of Jean Gerson (1363-1429) that mystical theology
is experimental knowledge of God through the embrace of unitive
love, and Bonaventure's dictum that mystical theology is the
raising of the mind to God through the desire of love.[10]
  While Dom Butler restricts the term mystical experience
to "that experimental perception of God, however expressed,
that is the real claim of the mystics in their higher states
of contemplation and union," and the term mystic to "the secret
knowledge or perception of God in contemplation,"[11] Evelyn

Underhill broadens the definition:

> Not only the act of contemplation, the vision or state
> of consciousness in which the soul of the great mystic
> realizes God, but many humbler and dimmer experiences of
> prayer, in which the little human spirit truly feels the
> presence of the divine spirit, and love must be included
> in it.... Every human soul has a certain latent capacity
> for God ... in some this capacity is realized with as-
> tonishing richness. Such a realization may be of many
> kinds and degrees--personal or impersonal, abrupt and
> ecstatic, or peaceful and continuous. This will depend
> partly on the temperament of the mystic, and partly on
> his religious background and education.[12]

In an even wider vein, Joseph Collins holds that "Mysticism
can be applied equally to all stages or ways of growth in the
spiritual life, even to the lower stages called ascetic, which
also contribute to the wholeness of the spiritual life and
unity of religious experience."[13] Christian mysticism then
can be viewed as the science concerned with the soul's journey
to God, via the threefold way of Purgation, Illumination, and
Union, the *via contemplativa*.

As defined by Dom David Knowles, following Hugh of St.
Victor, purgation is the purification of the self to God, a
process inherent in the ascetic life, which is generally but
not exclusively considered the first step toward the *via contemplativa*.[14] Illumination moves from prayerful meditation, a
discursive process which is an indispensable preparation for
the higher contemplative life, to contemplation, through which
the soul comes to know the truth of God and His Will, both for
the individual and for mankind. Contemplation, which can be
theocentric of Christocentric, acquired or infused, active or
passive, is the total spiritual process which leads to and may
culminate in the intimate union of the soul with God, an experience which is ineffable and indescribable.

Nor is the contemplative way restricted to a chosen few
religious solitaries: "While this gift [union] is in its ful-
ness the crown of the spiritual life, and the direct gift of
God alone, it should be the goal of all who seek God."[15] This
statement has a profound significance for the establishment
of the English mystical canon. As Hilton's work *On the Mixed
Life* reveals, the active and contemplative lives are not
mutually exclusive, for the active life incorporates both out-
ward works of charity and inward purgative exercises, which
can prepare a man for the contemplative life.[16] Similarly,
Dom Butler delineates two meanings for the contemplative life:
objectively, it is a manner of corporate life directed toward

promoting the exercise of contemplation, while subjectively,
a man leads a contemplative life who effectively practices
contemplation. Thus the contemplative life is a matter of
personal experience, not external conditions.[17] As S.S. Hussey
has also shown, Hilton's terms "active, contemplative and mixed"
are "psychological, not sociological, states and not estates."[18]

I am inclined to accept the broader and less restrictive
definition of mysticism as the progressive spiritual life of
the Christian from purgation through contemplation to unity.
The mystical canon then can feasibly include works concerned
with the methodology of mysticism, or with how to accomplish
these three stages,[19] as exemplified by the *Contemplations of
the Dread and Love of God*, which stresses purgation, *The Cloud
of Unknowing* and its attendant treatises, and Hilton's *Scale
of Perfection*. Yet this methodological emphasis slights the
two other main forms of mystical writing: the accounts of the
unitive experience itself and its significance, such as Julian's
Revelations; and prophetic visions, such as those of St. Birgitta of Sweden. It also fails to consider the mystics as
teachers, writing in the vernacular to promulgate the life of
perfection, but, even more, to edify and instruct not only the
professional clergy, but their "even Christians," the lay and
religious middle class.[20] As Dom Butler has observed, the sermon, the homily, the epistle, and the religious tract became
the mouthpieces of the mystics,[21] an enlargement of the mystical
corpus which would accommodate Richard Rolle's varied writings.

In arguing for this broad definition, I am reminded of the
time when Professor Ritamary Bradley and I were planning our
14th-Century English Mystics Newsletter, and Professor Siegfried Wenzel advised us to cover all Middle English devotional
literature, stating: "I cannot conceive of an effective newsletter on the medieval English mystics without including, say,
The Clensyng of Mannes Sowle, or, for that matter, the
Fasciculus Morum."[22] While sympathetic with his advice, we
realized the we would have to clarify and limit the mystical
corpus in order to facilitate its incorporation into a provisional schema for all of Middle English prose writings.
Assuredly, the formulation of such an overall scheme will be
necessary if the *Index* is to deal effectively with problems of
identification and classification of texts, decisions of which
texts to include or exclude, and subject indices, which, along
with the first-line index, are envisioned as the final stage of
the project. Such a scheme will not only be integral for the
ongoing phases of the *Index*, but also for interim related
projects, such as catalogues and bibliographies of specific
categories or works in Middle English prose, as, for example,
the published bibliography on the medieval English mystics, one
of a series published by Garland, the in-process revisions of

the Wells' *Manual*, and similar endeavors. As Professor A.S.G.
Edwards has indicated, such ancillary projects will not only
supplement and underpin the *Index*, but, closely linked to the
Index, will help to enhance its research potential.

Several attempts have been made to classify religious
texts by form and content. The Wells' *Manual* makes several
very broad divisions, with its "Rolle and His Followers" section attesting negatively to the growth of the mystical corpus
since the work was written.[23] More recently, Father Peter
Jolliffe, averring that there is no completely objective cri-
terion which can satisfactorily be employed, evolved a provisional schema of fifteen classifications for his *Checklist*,
which I feel are too narrow for the *Index*, and which, moreover,
exclude almost all of the mystical canon.[24] Joseph Milosh has
suggested the rather broad category of a religious handbook,
which would encompass instructions on asceticism and fundamental
Christian lore, but which again excludes contemplative or
speculatively theological works.[25] H.G. Pfander posits a
similar grouping of medieval manuals of religious instruction,
but, owing to their diversity, proposes a classification according to the language in which they were written.[26] Drawing
on the reform movements and flowering of devotional and mystical
works in the thirteenth and fourteenth centuries, W.A. Pantin
suggests three divisions: manuals for parish priests, vernacular
religious and moral treatises in the catechetical vein, and
mystical writings and religious lyrics. Pantin comments that
"the marked taste for mystical literature among the more devout
laity of the fourteenth and fifteenth centuries presupposes a
thorough grounding in dogmatic and moral instruction through
the pulpit, confessional, and reading."[27]

The most workable approach that I have found is outlined by
Professor N.F. Blake, who differentiates Middle English religious prose into five categories on the basis of the purpose
for which a particular text was written, since that purpose will
often determine the form and approach. His categories include:
(1) works designed for instruction, divided into primary instruction, straightforward explanation or teaching, and secondary instruction, written for the teaching and edification of
a more general audience; (2) works of an historical and legendary character; (3) affective works designed to stir up an
emotional response, which he admits is the weakest grouping;
(4) spiritual autobiographies, citing *The Book of Margery Kempe*;
and (5) polemic literature.[28] I favor this schema and especially Category 3, as it provides a broad framework for a
variety of works, the main purpose of which is to inculcate
and promote the progressive growth and perfection of spiritual
life.

At the same time, however, this approach may lead us into
subjective intentional fallacies, especially if works are

classified on the basis of a stated or implied audience. It
must be remembered, since both clergy and laity lacked theological knowledge, that "With vernacular texts ... it is not
always easy to be confident whether the audience addressed is
a lay audience or whether we have here a priest's manual in
his own language."[29] With regard to writings addressed to a
certain person, Helen Gardner, speaking of Book II of the *Scale
of Perfection*, states:

> It is not really necessary to assume that Hilton had
> anyone in mind for Book II. The habit of addressing
> some friend who had asked for instruction seems to have
> become a convention in mystical writings by the end of
> the fourteenth century.... Many of the anonymous mystical
> works of the period ... are also written to friends
> equally vague.[30]

Also, W.A. Pantin has observed:

> The vernacular mystical writings, while partially intended
> for the use of unlearned clerics and religious, including
> nuns and anchoresses, were also read by devout laypeople,
> owing to the most important phenomenon of the religious
> history of the later Middle Ages, namely, the rise of
> the devout and literate laymen ... [who] were enabled and
> encouraged to attempt the practice of contemplative
> prayer.[31]

A concomitant factor was the third orders, which permitted lay-
persons to participate in the life of religious orders, such
as the Franciscans and Dominicans. A similar point is made by
Elizabeth Salter, in her studies of English translations of
Ludolph of Saxony's *Vita Christi*:

> By the late fourteenth century, the provision of reli-
> gious texts in the vernacular may not have been simply
> for readers who could not understand Latin; the added
> convenience, but not always the necessity of studying or
> meditating in English is an important factor we should
> not overlook.[32]

I can offer no easy solution to the classification problem,
other than to suggest that, given their integral part in the
life of prayer and contemplation, affective meditations, and
especially those on the life and Passion of Christ, be allotted
a separate category on the border line of mystical writing.
This grouping could include meditations which are indebted to
thr popular pseudo-Bonaventuran mystical biography of Christ,
the *Meditationes Vitae Christi*, such as Nicholas Love's *Mirror*

of the *Blessed Life of Jesus*; the *Speculum Devotorum*; *The
Privity of the Passion*; *The Mirror of Our Lady*; the Anselmian
meditations *An Orison of Our Lord*, *A Lovesong of Our Lord*, and
The Wooing of Our Lord, with two of these latter works combined
and abridged into *The Talking of the Love of God*. Similarly,
treatises on the solitary life, such as Aelred of Rievaulx's
De Institutione Inclusarum, *Speculum Inclusorum*, the *Ancren
Riwle*, the Bridgettine *Rewyll of Seynt Saviore*, and Richard
Methley's *To Hew Heremyte: A Pystyl of Solytary Lyfe Nowadayes*,
should be adjacent to the mystics' writings, since, although
these works may emphasize theology and asceticism more than
mystical union, the aim of such a solitary vocation was to
achieve the *via contemplativa*.[33]

Further, following the lead of Father Edmund Colledge,[34]
the mystical category can also be extended to include such pre-
decessors as Aelred of Rievaulx's *Speculum Caritatis*, the lives
of Godric of Finchal and Christina of Markyate, Stephen of
Sawley's *Threefold Exercise*, Adam of Dryburgh's *Fourfold Exercise of the Cell*, and Edmund Rich's *Speculum Ecclesiae*. While
the majority of these works remained in their original Latin,
they represent a basis from which the fourteenth-century English
mystics proceeded, and, indeed, the later vernacular mystical
works can be evaluated properly only if viewed against the background of the tradition of Latin theology and mysticism.

I would suggest, therefore, that the mystical canon, in all
its variety of form and content, but united by its purpose of
promoting the attainment of the contemplative life, be classified *sui generis*, to include not only the works of the five
major figures, but also Middle English translations of Latin
mystical texts composed in England and on the Continent, as
well as translations of continental vernacular works, and rep-
resentatives of the ongoing tradition, mainly the works of
Richard Whytford, Augustine Baker, and the recusant religious,
up to Benet Canfield. One cannot, of course, overlook
lesser-known native English additions to the mystical canon,
such as John Alcock's *Mons Perfectionis*, known as *The Hill of
Perfection*, a sermon on the contemplative life addressed to the
Carthusians at the Charterhouse of St. Anne in Coventry; *The
Tree and XII Fruits of the Holy Ghost*; *The Abbey of the Holy
Ghost*, written to show how a devout layperson can live in a
spiritual convent while remaining in the world,[35] and *Contemplations of the Dread and Love of God*, both reminiscent of Hilton's
Mixed Life; and the mystical portions of such popular compen-
diums as the *Speculum Spiritualium*, *Disce Mori*, *Pore Caitif*,
and *Tretyse of Love*.

Turning now to specific problems relating to mystical works,
I would first like to address their complex translation process.
A major part of the secondary writings of this canon is comprised

of English translations of continental works, accomplished in
great measure, as Father Edmund Colledge and others have shown,
by the Carthusians at the London Charterhouse, Sheen, and Mount
Grace, and by the Bridgettines of Syon Abbey.

Of the German mystics of the *Gottesfreunde/devotio moderna*
movements, Henry Suso was the most popular, although the *Index*
manuscript search may uncover English translations of Meister
Eckhart and Tauler, along with the later continental mystics
Jean Gerson and Nicholas of Cusa. Suso's *Büchlein der ewigen
Weisheit*, widely diffused in the Middle Ages, was translated
into the Latin *Horologium Sapientiae*, thence into the English
*Treatys of the Sevene Poyntes of Trewe Love and Everlastynge
Wisdom*. Two of the major works of the great Flemish mystic,
Jan van Ruysbroeck, were translated into Latin, then English:
Van den blinkenden Steen into the *Treatise of Perfection of
the Sons of God*, and *Die Geestelijke Brülocht* into the *Chastising of God's Children*. If the *Imitation of Christ* can be
classified as a mystical work, and Dorothy Jones feels that it
should be,[36] it would join the abovementioned translations,
and again via Carthusian transmission.

The works of leading female continental mystics were also
translated into Middle English. St. Birgitta of Sweden's
Revelations were "Englished" for the Syon nuns, as was St.
Catherine of Siena's *Dialogo*, entitled *The Orchard of Syon*.
Her Latin *Lyf* was translated into English and printed in 1493.
There are also Middle English prose legends of three thirteenth-
century ecstatics, all within the *Brautmystik* tradition: St.
Elizabeth of Spaelbeck, St. Christina Mirabilis, and St. Mary
of Oegines. Hope Emily Allen not only referred to the English
translation of Mechthild of Hackborn's *Book of Spiritual Grace*,
which she identified with the *Mauldebuke*, but also proposed to
undertake a study of unedited fifteenth-century English translations from continental works of feminine piety, to adduce
the influence of these writings on the native mystical tradition.[37] It is to be regretted that she could not pursue this
study, but here is an additional area where the *Index* search
may bear fruit. Yet another work by a continental woman mystic,
The Mirror of Simple Souls, written by Margaret Porete, was
translated from French into English and glossed by one "M.N."
in the middle or late fourteenth century.

Among other continental Latin writings which were translated *in toto* or incorporated into Middle English mystical
works were the *Scala Paradisi* or *Scala Claustralium*, attributed
to Guigo II of the Grand Chartreuse, and appearing in the late
fourteenth or early fifteenth century as *A Ladder of Foure
Ronges by the Whiche Men Mowe Wele Clyme to Heven*, also called
The Laddyr of Cloystrerys and *Scala Celi*; Alphone of Pecha's
Epistola Solitarii, the Latin compilation *Quandoque Tributaris*

Vel Temptaris, and the *Stimulus Amoris*, all incorporated into
The Chastising of God's Children; Hugh of Balma's *Viae Sion
Lugent* or *De Triplici Via* or *De Mystica Theologia*, included in
two Middle English Carthusian compilations on the contemplative
life: *Of actyfe lyfe and contemplatyf declaracion* and *Via ad
contemplacion*; James of Milan's *Stimulus Amoris*, reputedly
translated by Walter Hilton as *The Prick or Goad of Love*; Hilton's *Eight Chapters of Perfection*, translated from a work by
Louis de Fontibus; Peter of Blois' *Duodecim Utilitates Tribu-
lationes*, which became *The Twelve Profits of Tribulation*; Peter
Lombard's *Commentarium on Psalmos*, thought to have informed
Richard Rolle's *Commentary on the Psalter*; Etienne de Salley's
Speculum Novitii, which was the basis for Rolle's *On Daily Work*;
pseudo-Dionysius' *Mystica Theologia* and Richard of St. Victor's
Benjamin Minor, translated by the *Cloud* author into *Deonise
Hid Divinite* and *A Treatyse of þe Stodye of Wysdome þat Men
Clepen Beniamyn*; and Ludolph of Saxony's *Vita Christi*, which
emerged as *The Mirrour or Glasse of Christes Passioun*.

   Latin works written in England and translated into Middle
English also swelled the mystical corpus. Aelred of Rievaulx's
De Institutione Inclusarum was "Englished" in the fourteenth
century, under the title *Informacio Aelredi Abbatis Monasterij
de Rievalli ad Sororem Suam Inclusarum*; Edmund Rich's influen-
tial *Speculum Ecclesie*, entitled *Mirror of Holy Church*, stressing the three ways to contemplate God, occurred not only in a
complete fourteenth-century English version, but in two derivative works, the *Prick of Love* in verse, and *How a man shall
live perfectly*, excerpted from the first part of the *Mirror*.
William Flete's ascetical treatise *De Remediis Contra Tempta-
ciones*, written before his departure for Italy in 1359, appeared
in three Middle English versions. Two of Richard Rolle's works,
Incendium Amoris and *De Emendatione Vitae*, were translated by
Richard Misyn into *The Fire of Love* and *Mending of Life* respectively, while Richard Whytford translated the *Imitatio Christi*
into English.

   Just as these Latin works were translated into the vernacular to reach a broader audience, so certain of the Middle
English treatises were translated into Latin, in order to gain
the approbation of readers in religious orders. Thus in 1490
Richard Methley translated both *The Cloud of Unknowing* and the
"M.N." version of *The Mirror of Simple Souls* into Latin, adding
his own glosses to obscure or possibly heterodox portions of
the latter work.[38] Joy Russell-Smith has also suggested that
the writings of the fourteenth-century contemplative writers
may have been closely scrutinized by theologians, thereby ac-
counting for the Carmelite Thomas Fishlake's Latin translation
of both books of *The Scale of Perfection* "per quendam sacre
theologie doctore," before 1400.[39]

In the light of this rather complex translation pattern, I
note in the "Preliminary Procedures for the Preparation of
Index Handlists" that rubrics in English preceding works in
other languages and material primarily in another language will
not be indexed, but will be noted. While I realize that the
Index cannot encompass the entire medieval manuscript corpus,
I do feel that the aforementioned category of translated mystical texts underscores the importance of including brief descriptions of non-English texts, both Latin and vernacular, and their
titles and incipits. There are several scholarly benefits to
be gained from such a procedure, in the areas of textual criticism, measuring the impact and influence which the translators
of these works had on the development of English prose, and
assessing the religious temper of the age. For example, an
examination of the "M.N." and Methley glosses on *The Mirror
of Simple Souls*, both of which avoid Porete's suspect comments
on the hypostatic union, reveals "the low ebb of Christological
learning in the late medieval church."[40] As has been shown in
the case of Flete's *De Remediis*, Edmund Rich's *Speculum
Ecclesie*, and Porete's *Mirror*, a thorough study of the Latin
and vernacular manuscript tradition is essential in order to
evolve the original text and accretive versions. It must also
be kept in mind that several of Rolle's more mystical works
were in Latin and were not translated, as was the case with
Richard Methley's *Scola Amoris Languidi* and *Experimentum Veri-
tatis* on the contemplative life. Still another benefit is the
possibility of uncovering a larger Anglo-Latin mystical corpus
to which the mystical meditations of the Monk-Solitary of
Farne testify.[41] Similarly, the noting and brief descriptions
of French and particularly Anglo-Norman texts would further
the consideration of these writings, both as heralds of the
English mystical movement of the fourteenth century and as an
integral part of the medieval literary corpus, a consideration
which, as suggested by Hope Emily Allen, is long overdue.[42]

Turning now to the fourth problem area, I would like to
urge that the indexers carefully note titles and rubrics, or
lack of same. This would address several related problems which
are not unique to mystical manuscripts, but are of great importance, namely, false ascriptions, multiple titles or none, and
the excerpt/compilation/emendation/interpolation processes,
as delineated below.

With regard to false ascriptions, in the thirteenth century,
for instance, Robert Grosseteste was erroneously credited with
many works, including the *Peines of Purgatorie*. This same
process of attribution continued in the fourteenth and fifteenth
centuries, enlarging Richard Rolle's already sizeable output to
include many Latin treatises and English works, such as Edmund
Rich's *Mirror*, Flete's *De Remediis*, several anonymous Passion

meditations,[43] and, although not in prose, the *Pricke of Conscience*. While the seminal work of Hope Emily Allen and Geraldine Hodgson has established the Rolle canon, further manuscript study may augment their findings.[44] As if in retaliation, Rolle's *Incendium Amoris* was erroneously assigned to St. Bonaventure.[45] Walter Hilton was credited with the first three books of the *Imitation of Christ*, Ruysbroeck's *Chastising of God's Children*,[46] and, according to the Carthusian John Grenehalgh, one of the most respected editors of mystical manuscripts, *The Cloud of the Unknowing*, an ascription which has become a crux in the problem of the *Cloud*'s authorship. Such attributions may be due to the medieval love of authority, the esteem with which these authors were regarded, or, in some instances, contiguity with other of their works in a given manuscript, but nevertheless complicate efforts to establish definitive canons.

Possibly an even greater problem arises from the lack of an ascription or title, which the *Index* survey may find accounts for numerous heretofore "anonymous" works. A converse complication is too many titles, making it difficult to assign or identify spiritual texts, as the following examples will attest. Flete's *De Remediis* is known as *A good remedie agens spiritual temptacion* and *Consolacio Animae*. *Contemplations of the Dread and Love of God*, a title given by Wynkyn de Worde, is called *Ffervor Amoris, XII Chapters, De Quattro Gradibus Amoris, Amor Dei, The Love of God, Tractatus Divini Amoris*, and *Of the direction of a man's life*. *The Scale of Perfection* is called *De Nobilitate Animae*. Book I of the English version is at times entitled *Prima Pars Libri Qui Dicitur Speculum Contemplacionis*, while in the Latin translation it is called *Libellus Primus Magistri Walter Hylton* and *Tractatus De Arte Bene Vivendi*. Book II is identified as *þe secunde part of þe reformyng of mannys soul drawyn of maister Walter Hilton hermyte*. In fact, the title *Scala Perfectionis* occurs only when both books are present. The *Pore Caitif* merits *Pauper Rusticus* or *Confessio Derelicti Pauperis*. *Benjamin Minor* is called the *Boke of the XII Patriarkys*, while the *Imitation of Christ* circulated in England as *De Ecclesiastica Musica*. In the same vein, countless examples can be given for differing incipits for the same works. In this category of problems, the worth and even the necessity for carefully noting rubrics and incipits should be manifest.

The *Index* search will undoubtedly produce further evidence of the processes of excerption, compilation, emendation, and interpolation which mark the mystical texts throughout the Middle Ages and beyond. This knowledge will permit further scholarly research on sources and influences, and also facilitate the preparation of critical texts. In this area, as with false ascriptions, Richard Rolle appears to be unduly favored, as his writings were continually broken up into parts, joined together in different combinations, or subsumed into larger works. For example, *Form of Living* passages appear in Watton's *Speculum Christiani* and in the *Speculum Spiritualium*.[47] Other Rolle compilations are the *De Excellentia Contemplationis* and the well-known *Quandoque Tribularis* gathering.[48] Direct or indirect quotation from Flete's *De Remediis* appear in *An Epistle for the Discerning of Spirits* and the *Speculum Christiani*, both of the fourteenth century, and in various versions of the *Contemplations of the Dread and Love of God*, *Speculum Spiritualium*, and *Donatus Devotionis*, all of the fifteenth century.[49] Particularly representative of the borrowing process in spiritual compilations are *Of actyfe lyfe and contemplatyf declaracion* and *Via ad Contemplacion*, which not only combine Hugh of Balma's *Mystica Theologia*, but also selections from the *Scale* and the *Cloud* corpus.[50] The *Pore Caitif* contains, among its fourteen tracts, two fragments of the *Ancren Riwle*, while its middle section, "Some short sentences exciting men to heavenly desire," may possibly have been drawn from a Rolle text.[51] The foregoing are but a few illustrations of a widespread practice, and one which the *Index* could well bring into its deserved scholarly focus.

In addition to compilations, the mystical texts underwent continuous emendations. What Helen Gardner points out about *The Scale of Perfection* holds true for similar works as well. A study of the *Scale* manuscripts shows that it was revised and adapted almost from its first appearance to make it fulfill the purpose of edification for which it was originally intended.[52] The many problems presented by the manuscript tradition of the *Scale*, insofar as the Christocentric additions and the evolving of a critical edition are concerned, have been carefully examined by Helen Gardner and S.S. Hussey,[53] and the *Index*'s findings may well provide further answers to these problems. Other illustrations of the emendation process on which the *Index* explorations can shed light are the three accretive English versions of Flete's *De Remediis*; the Lollard interpolations in manuscripts of Rolle's *Psalter*, as pointed out by Dorothy Everett;[54] the incorporation of Rolle's writings into some mystical lyrics;[55] and, as N.F. Blake has shown, the practice of versifying Rolle's and other prose treatises, in many instances excising the more mystical material in order to transform the work into a more broadly devotional piece, suitable for a general lay audience.[56] And, according to T.A. Birrell, emendations of these medieval writings continued not only in the exiled recusant communities, but in post-Reformation England, with these latter adaptations marked by the removal of "Popish error."[57]

Although Helen White posits the elimination of the contemplative book in England, owing to the Reformation,[58] Joseph
Collins maintains that an interest in the English medieval
mystical writings continued through the turn of the sixteenth
century and a few decades thereafter.[59]   In addition, during
this same period, *Deonise Hid Divinite* and Margery Kempe's *A
Short Treatyse of Contemplacyon* were published by Wynkyn de
Worde, and Hilton's works enjoyed continued popularity.   These
facts support the *Index*'s planned search of post-1500 manuscripts.   In England, however, the dissolution and subsequent
diaspora of monastic communities and their libraries resulted
either in the loss of manuscripts or their passing into the
private sector for safekeeping--the prime example of this latter occurrence being *The Book of Margery Kempe*, which was left
by Mount Grace Charterhouse to the Butler-Bowden family and
rediscovered only in 1934.[60]   Dorothy Jones indicated a late
seventeenth-century manuscript of the *Scale* in the library
catalogues of Sir Thomas Philippe.[61]   More recently, James Hogg
located a text of Richard Methley's *To Hew Heremyte* in the London Public Record Office,[62] while Michael Sargent, acting on
the advice of Dr. A.I. Doyle, explored the Walker-Heneage
(Button) Collection at the Somerset Record Office at Taunton,
and found unnoticed copies of three Middle English prose
spiritual works, including a text of *The Chastising of God's
Children* ascribed to Walter Hilton.[63]   R.M. Wilson has eloquently
supported the examination of wills and catalogues of monastic
and other smaller public and private libraries, while cautioning
that this activity is complicated by the rather general nature
of many of the catalogues and the lack of knowledgeable library
personnel.[64]   Yet invaluable headway has been made by Margaret
Deansley's survey of vernacular books in some 7,600 English
wills of the fourteenth and fifteenth centuries,[65] E. Margaret
Thompson's lists of manuscripts and printed books in the Carthusian Charterhouses,[66] Mary Bateson's catalogue of Syon
library holdings,[67] and, above all, Dr. A.I. Doyle's monumental
survey of the origins and circulation of theological writings
in the fourteenth, fifteenth, and sixteenth centuries.[68]

    In considering the preservation and transmission of medieval
mystical texts in England before the Reformation and on the Continent after that event, one cannot overemphasize the importance
of the Carthusians, the Bridgettines of Syon Abbey, and the
Benedictines.   At the Benedictine contemplative community and
scriptorium at Cambrai, for example, English spiritual writings
were not only brought over and copied, as Father Augustine
Baker's well-known letter to Sir Robert Cotton attests, but
derivative works were compiled by religious at Cambrai and
other houses.   Of special note are Father Baker's *Sancta Sophia*,
his recension, with commentary, of the *Cloud*, and modernization

of the *De Remediis*; Dame Gertrude More's *Confessiones Amantis*; and the extensive editing and publishing work of Father Serenus Cressy.[69] And although the returning religious brought some of their manuscripts with them, others were lost, and presumably are extant on the Continent. Just how great this loss factor was may be determined from surviving library catalogues of the Shene Anglorum Charterhouse, and Paris and Cambrai Benedictine houses, lists which manifest how highly these exiled contemplatives valued their native spiritual heritage and its mystical texts.[70]

Much ground work has been done on the search for and assessment of continental holdings of mystical texts by such scholars as Helen Gardner,[71] Hope Emily Allen,[72] Anna Paues,[73] Dom Justin McCann,[74] Dom Placid Spearitt,[75] and T.A. Birrell,[76] to mention only a few. Their work clearly indicates the research potential of this corpus, and supports the *Index*'s plan to enlist the aid of continental scholars to complement the present cadre of British and North American indexers.

I have attempted to summarize special problems, research opportunities, and recommendations for the *Index of Middle English Prose* regarding the English mystics, and will welcome comments and suggestions in any or all of these areas. So far as the mystics are concerned, I feel that the *Index* will encourage and facilitate important research on a truly interdisciplinary basis, for the material is of interest to literary scholars, historians, philologists, philosophers, and theologians. Moreover, it should help to produce critical editions which are badly needed, not only as scholarly tools, but also for the dissemination of the English mystics' timeless message of hope and love to ongoing generations. As a scholar of the mystics, I am very enthusiastic about the *Index*, and am honored to join with you in this international venture, which, in my estimation, is the most important medieval research project of our era.

Valerie M. Lagorio
University of Iowa

NOTES

1. Dom Cuthbert Butler, *Western Mysticism* (London, 1922; rpt. 1927), p. 1.

2. Evelyn Underhill, *Mystics of the Church* (New York, 1964), p. 17.

3. Evelyn Underhill, "Two Franciscan Mystics: Jacopone da Todi and Angela of Foligno," in *St. Francis of Assisi: 1226-1926: Essays in Commemoration*, ed. Walter Seton (London, 1926), p. 313.

4. Anna Groh Seesholtz, *Friends of God. Practical Mystics of the Fourteenth Century* (New York, 1934), p. 26.

5. Dom David Knowles, *The English Mystical Tradition* (New York, 1961), p. 193.

6. Butler, op. cit., p. 2.

7. Phyllis Hodgson, *Three Fourteenth-Century English Mystics* (London, 1967), p. 9.

8. Underhill, *Mystics of the Church*, p. 10.

9. William Johnston, *The Inner Eye of Love* (London, 1978), p. 43.

10. Ibid., p. 19.

11. Butler, op. cit, p. lxxiv.

12. Underhill, *Mystics of the Church*, p. 9.

13. Joseph Collins, *Christian Mysticism in the Elizabethan Age* (Baltimore, Md., 1940; rpt. New York, 1971), p. viii.

14. Knowles, op. cit., p. 31; Hugh of St. Victor, *Selected Spiritual Writings*, tr. by Religious of C.S.M.V., with Introduction by Aelred Squire (New York and Evanston, 1962), p. 183.

15. Walter Hilton, *The Ladder of Perfection*, tr. by Leo Sherley-Price (London, 1957), p. xx.

16. Joy Russell-Smith, "Walter Hilton," *The Month*, n.s. 21 (1959), 136.

17. Butler, op. cit., p. 290.

18. S.S. Hussey, "Langland, Hilton, and the Three Lives," *Review of English Studies*, n.s. 7 (1956), 133; also see Walter H. Beale, "Walter Hilton and the Concept of 'Medled Lyf,'" *American Benedictine Review*, 26 (1975), 381-94, for a further discussion of the medieval significance of the terms "active" and "contemplative."

19. Collins, op. cit., p. 2.

20. Underhill, *Mystics of the Church*, p. 110.

21. Butler, op. cit., pp. xii-xiii.

22. *14th-Century English Mystics Newsletter*, I/1 (1974).

23. John Edwin Wells, *A Manual of the Writings in Middle English* (New Haven, 1916), Chap. VI, pp. 338-73, and Chap. XI, pp. 444-64.

24. Fr. Peter Jolliffe, *A Checklist of Middle English Prose Writings of Spiritual Guidance* (Toronto, 1974), pp. 11-57.

25. Joseph E. Milosh, *The Scale of Perfection and the English Mystical Tradition* (Madison, Wisc., 1966), pp. 140-50.

26. H.G. Pfander, "Some Medieval Manuals of Religious Instruction in England and Observations on Chaucer's Parson's Tale," *JEGP*, 35 (1936), 243-58.

27. W.A. Pantin, *The English Church in the Fourteenth Century* (Notre Dame, Ind., 1962), pp. 189-92.

28. N.F. Blake, "Varieties of Middle English Religious Prose," in *Chaucer and Middle English Studies*, ed. Beryl Rowland (London, 1974), pp. 348-56.

29. G.H. Russell, "Vernacular Instruction of the Laity in the Later Middle Ages in England: Some Texts and Notes," *Journal of Religious History*, 2 (1962), 100.

30. Helen Gardner, "The Text of *The Scale of Perfection*," *Medium Aevum*, 5 (1936), 15.

31. Pantin, op. cit., p. 254.

32. Elizabeth Salter, "Ludolphus of Saxony and His English Translators," *Medium Aevum*, 33 (1964), 29.

33. Nancy A. Hunt, "Sloth in a Guide for Contemplatives, the *Ancrene Riwle*," *Counterpoint* (Spring 1974), p. 66.

34. Edmund Colledge, ed., *The Mediaeval Mystics of England* (New York, 1961), pp. 5-55.

35. Pantin, op. cit., pp. 253-54; Peter Consacro, "The Author of *The Abbey of the Holy Ghost*: A Popularizer of the Mixed Life," *14th-Century English Mystics Newsletter*, II/4 (1976), 15-20.

36. Dorothy Jones, *Minor Works of Walter Hilton* (London, 1929), p. xlviii. William Fairweather, *Among the Mystics* (Edinburgh, 1936), p. 33, also refers to the "mystical piety" of the *Imitation*.

37. Sanford B. Meech and H.E. Allen, eds., *The Book of Margery Kempe*, EETS, o.s. 212 (London, 1940), Vol. I, pp. lxi-lxviii. Also see Theresa Halligan, "The Revelations of St. Mathilde in English: *The Booke of Gostlye Grace*," *Notes and Queries*, 219 (1974), 443-46.

38. Marilyn Doiron, ed., "Margaret Porete, *The Mirror of Simple Souls*: A Middle English Translation," *Archivio Italiano per la Storia della Pietà*, 5 (1968), 241-355, and Appendix, E. Colledge and R. Guarnieri, "The Glosses by 'M.N.' and Richard Methley to *The Mirror of Simple Souls*," 357-82.

39. Russell-Smith, op. cit., p. 143.

40. Doiron, op. cit., p. 90.

41. W.A. Pantin, "The Monk-Solitary of Farne," *English Historical Review*, 59 (1944), 162-86; Hugh Farmer, ed., *The Monk of Farne* (Baltimore, Md., 1961).

42. Hope Emily Allen, "The Mystical Lyrics of the *Manuel des Pechiez*," *Romanic Review*, 9 (1918), 154-93.

43. Harry W. Robbins, "An English Version of St. Edmund's *Mirror*, Ascribed to Richard Rolle," *PMLA*, 40 (1925), 240-51; Margery M. Morgan, "Versions of the Meditations on the Passion Ascribed to Richard Rolle," *Medium Aevum*, 22 (1953), 93-103; Carl Horstman, *Yorkshire Writers* II (London, 1896), p. xxxix.

44. Hope Emily Allen, *Writings Ascribed to Richard Rolle, Hermit of Hampole, and Materials for His Biography*, Modern Language Assn. of America Monograph Series III (London, 1927); G.E. Hodgson, *Some Minor Works of Richard Rolle* (London, 1923) and *Rolle and Our Daily Work* (London, 1929).

45. Margaret Deansley, "The *Incendium Amoris* of Richard Rolle and St. Bonaventura," *English Historical Review*, 29 (1914), 98-99.

46. Michael Sargent, "A New Manuscript of *The Chastising of God's Children*, with an Ascription to Walter Hilton," *Medium Aevum*, 46 (1977), 49.

47. Horstman, op. cit., p. xl.

48. Michael Sargent, "The Transmission by the English Carthusians of Some Late Medieval Spiritual Writings," *Journal of Ecclesiastical History*, 27 (1976), 231-32.

49. Benedict Hackett, "William Flete," in *Pre-Reformation Spirituality*, ed. James Walsh (London, 1965), p. 164.

50. Fr. Peter Jolliffe, "Two Middle English Tracts on the Contemplative Life," *Mediaeval Studies*, 37 (1975), 86-87.

51. Sargent, "The Transmission by the English Carthusians of Some Late Medieval Spiritual Writings," p. 232; see also Sr. Mary Theresa Brady, "The *Pore Caitif*. An Introductory Study," *Traditio*, 10 (1954), 529-48.

52. Gardner, op. cit., p. 12.

53. S.S. Hussey, "The Text of *The Scale of Perfection*, Book II," *Neuphilologische Mitteilungen*, 65 (1964), 90.

54. Dorothy Everett, "The Middle English Prose Psalter of Richard Rolle of Hampole," *Modern Language Review*, 18 (1923), 381-93.

55. Hope Emily Allen, "On Richard Rolle's Lyrics," *Modern Language Review*, 14 (1919), 320-21; Frances M.M. Comper, *The Life of Richard Rolle Together with an Edition of His English Lyrics* (London, 1928; rpt. New York, 1969), pp. 222 ff.

56. N.F. Blake, "*The Form of Living* in Prose and Poetry," *Archiv für das Studium der neueren Sprachen und Literatur*, 211 (1974), 300-08.

57. T.A. Birrell, "English Catholic Mystics in Non-Catholic Circles," *Downside Review*, 94 (1976), 60-81.

58. Helen White, "Some Continuing Traditions in English Devotional Literature," *PMLA*, 57 (1942), 968.

59. Collins, op. cit., pp. 79-80.

60. Meech and Allen, op. cit., p. xxxii. Ms. Allen identified the manuscript as Margery's *Book*.

61. Jones, op. cit., pp. ix-x.

62. James Hogg, ed., *Richard Methley: To Hew Heremyte A Pystyl of Solytary Lyfe Nowadayes*. Analecta Cartusiana, 31 (Salzburg, 1977), p. 235.

63. Sargent, "A New Manuscript of *The Chastising of God's Children*," p. 49.

64. R.M. Wilson, *The Lost Literature of Medieval England* (London, 1952; 2d. ed., 1970), pp. 135-58; cf. also Dom Placid Spearitt, "The Survival of Mediaeval Spirituality Among the Exiled Black Monks," *American Benedictine Review*, 25 (1974), 306.

65. Margaret Deansley, "Vernacular Books in England in the Fourteenth and Fifteenth Centuries," *Modern Language Review*, 15 (1920), 349-58.

66. Margaret Thompson, *The Carthusian Order in England* (London, 1930).

67. Mary Bateson, *Catalogue of the Library of Syon Monastery* (Cambridge, 1898).

68. A.I. Doyle, "A Survey of the Origins and Circulation of Theological Writings in English in the Fourteenth, Fifteenth and Early Sixteenth Centuries with Special Consideration of the Part of the Clergy Therein," Cambridge Ph.D. Dissertation (1954), 2301-2302.

69. For thorough studies of the Cambrai community, see Spearitt, op. cit.; Birrell, op. cit.; Pater Salvin and Serenus Cressy, *The Life of Augustine Baker, O.S.B. (1575-1641)*, ed. Justin McCann (London, 1933); Anthony Low, *Augustine Baker* (New York, 1970).

70. Marion Norman, "Dame Gertrude More and the English Mystical Tradition," *Recusant History*, 13 (1976), 127.

71. Gardner, op. cit., p. 11.

72. Allen, *Writings*, pp. 22-50, 563-68, 396; see also Knowles, op. cit., pp. 65 ff.

73. Eilert Ekwall, "The MS Collections of the Late Professor Anna Paues," *Studia Neophilologica*, 21 (1948-49), 23-41.

74. McCann, op. cit., pp. 160-201; *Catholic Record Society*, 33 (1933), 274-93; and "Ten More Baker Manuscripts," *Ampleforth Journal*, 63 (1958), 77-83.

75. Spearitt, op. cit., pp. 307-08.

76. Birrell, op. cit., pp. 60, 99-117, 213-31; cf. also Norman, op. cit., p. 196.